NEW YORK'S
HISTORIC RESTAURANTS, INNS & TAVERNS

STORIED ESTABLISHMENTS

from the CITY *to the* HUDSON VALLEY

LAURA BRIENZA

D1301524

Globe
Pequot

Guilford, Connecticut

Globe
Pequot

An imprint of Rowman & Littlefield

Distributed by NATIONAL BOOK NETWORK

Copyright © 2016 by Laura Brienza

British Library Cataloguing in Publication Information Available

Library of Congress Cataloging-in-Publication Data

Names: Brienza, Laura, 1988- author.
Title: New York's historic restaurants, inns & taverns : storied
  establishments from the City to the Hudson Valley / Laura Brienza.
Other titles: New York's historic restaurants, inns and taverns
Description: Guilford, CT : Globe Pequot, [2016] | Includes bibliographical
  references and index.
Identifiers: LCCN 2016019321 (print) | LCCN 2016020000 (ebook) | ISBN
  9781493024346 (paperback : alkaline paper) | ISBN 9781493024353 (ebook) |
  ISBN 9781493024353 (Electronic)
Subjects: LCSH: Restaurants—New York (State)—New York—Guidebooks. |
  Restaurants—Hudson River Valley (N.Y. and N.J.)—Guidebooks. | Taverns
  (Inns)—New York (State)—New York—Guidebooks. | Taverns (Inns)—Hudson
  River Valley (N.Y. and N.J.)—Guidebooks. | Historic buildings—New York
  (State)—New York—Guidebooks. | Historic buildings—Hudson River Valley
  (N.Y. and N.J.)—Guidebooks. | New York (N.Y.)—Buildings, structures,
  etc.—Guidebooks. | Hudson River Valley (N.Y. and N.J.)—History, Local. |
  New York N.Y.)—Guidebooks. | Hudson River Valley (N.Y. and
  N.J.)—Guidebooks.
Classification: LCC TX907.3.N72 N4256 2016 (print) | LCC TX907.3.N72 (ebook)
  | DDC 647.95747—dc23
LC record available at https://lccn.loc.gov/2016019321

CONTENTS

INTRODUCTION

Big things happen over food or drink. Lives are changed. History is made. J.K. Rowling first penned *Harry Potter* at a café. Patriots cooked up the Boston Tea Party in a bar. I wrote this book at Starbucks.

We take grabbing a drink at the local pub or enjoying dinner at a restaurant for granted. But this was once a novel idea. The infrastructure did not always exist. We can trace the concept of the restaurant to ancient Rome. Romans did not cook at home but instead used a common area in the community to prepare food. Eating outside of the home was a necessity. The creation of inns and taverns followed.

England created tipping in the seventeenth century. Establishments displayed jars labeled T.I.P. for "To Insure Promptness." Patrons filled them with money to incentivize quality job performance. The tip jar concept journeyed across the pond to the United States in the late nineteenth century. An article from *The New York Times* in 1897 criticized the addition as "the vilest of imported vices," arguing that it created a lower class financially dependent on a higher class's generosity. Today's servers hustling without a legal guarantee of tips might agree.

When the British colonists built infrastructure in the New World, the first building they erected was usually a tavern. These were not just places to have a drink. They functioned more like convention centers: places for people to share ideas, complain, organize, and create change. People from all walks of life mixed together at the local tavern. In fact, laws actually declared a maximum charge for drinks, making sure that all were able to enter. (Of course, this idea of egalitarianism extended only to all classes of *white men*.) Taverns became the earliest form of assembly, ingraining Americans with the belief that they had an innate right to assemble and exercise freedom of speech.

It is fitting, then, that the American Revolution began in a bar. Fed up colonists planned the Boston Tea Party in the Green Dragon. And the Boston Tea Party's lame cousin, the New York Tea Party, originated in Manhattan's Fraunces Tavern. The American Revolution, the Whisky Rebellion, and the Stonewall Riots were all born in bars.

Politics and taverns have had a long marriage. In her book *America Walks Into A Bar*, Christine Sismondo argues that Prohibition functioned as a political means to disenfranchise blacks and immigrants from organizing in bars. If those already in power could prohibit immigrants and minorities from gathering in bars (and subsequently organizing for better treatment), they could maintain the status quo, keeping themselves in power. Moreover, closing taverns on Sunday targeted the lower classes. Most poor people worked six days a week. Sunday was their only day off. If the taverns were closed, they couldn't drink or organize. Moreover, some taverns that continued to operate during Prohibition usually raised their prices, making them inaccessible to lower classes.

The concept of the restaurant as we know it is relatively new. Yes, taverns and inns provided food. But there was no such thing as a menu. In general, everybody got the same thing for the same price. But after the French monarchy fell in 1792, royal cooks in need of new jobs opened the first known restaurants, offering a novel concept of food à la carte. Burger King was decades away, but "Have It Your Way" had been born. Restaurants spread to the United States in the early nineteenth century.

New York has many historic watering holes and eateries. This book will profile some of the state's most historic restaurants, inns, and taverns, focusing on New York City and the Hudson Valley. We'll focus on establishments that have been in operation for about a century, although I've made some exceptions. You will discover the most storied culinary establishments in all five boroughs and sail up the Hudson River, stopping at its most interesting bed and breakfasts, bars, and restaurants.

You'll travel to the tavern where George Washington hosted a farewell dinner for his officers at the close of the American Revolution. At this same tavern, you'll learn about the black men who fought for the British and came here to prove their loyalty to the Royal Crown. Doing so meant free passage to a life of liberty in Great Britain.

You'll eat steak at some of the city's oldest steakhouses and pizza at the country's first pizzeria. You'll have a cocktail at two bars where the fight for LGBT equality began. You'll rest your head in one of the original houses built by Dutch colonists in the Hudson Valley.

So get your appetite for great food and savory history ready. Then turn the page.

A BRIEF HISTORY OF
NEW YORK CITY

In the iconic words of Frank Sinatra, New York is "a city that doesn't sleep." An overcrowded, competitive jungle, if you can make it in New York City, you can "make it anywhere." The nineteenth century saw an explosion of immigration as America, and specifically New York, became synonymous with opportunity. The Statue of Liberty, dedicated in 1886, welcomed immigrants to a new life. The French gave the statue to the United States to celebrate their shared values of liberty. But the statue became a symbol of the commitment to diversity in the United States when the city engraved the poem "New Colossus" by Emma Lazarus on the statue's pedestal in 1903. The sonnet's most famous lines are:

> *Give me your tired, your poor,*
> *Your huddled masses yearning to breathe free,*
> *The wretched refuse of your teeming shore.*
> *Send these, the homeless, tempest-tost to me,*
> *I lift my lamp beside the golden door!*

Lady Liberty's fame spread among immigrants across the seas. She took on new significance as the "Mother of Exiles." Twentieth-century immigrants sailing in to Ellis Island knew to look for the sight of this statue as a symbol of new beginnings.

Indeed, New York is where people come to start over, to reinvent themselves, to pursue their dreams. As Jay Z raps in "Empire State of Mind," "these streets will make you feel brand new / big lights will inspire you." Taylor Swift, New York's Global Tourism Ambassador for 2014–2015, describes

the city as a place where everybody "wanted something more / searching for a sound we hadn't heard before" in her song "Welcome to New York." She comments on New York's enthusiasm for those who march to the beat of their own drum, particularly people who might be ostracized in other areas due to race, religion, or sexual orientation: "Everybody here was someone else before / And you can want who you want / Boys and boys and / Girls and girls." While New York is certainly not a utopia free from discrimination, its diverse population has offered a welcome contrast to homogeneous populations in other parts of the country or world.

Today, New York City includes five boroughs: Manhattan, Brooklyn, Queens, the Bronx, and Staten Island. These districts amass about 305 square miles and hold around 8.5 million people according to the 2014 census. But modern New York City began with a settlement of about thirty

Dutch families in 1624 following the Dutch East India Company's exploration of the area. The Dutch purchased Manhattan from Native Americans for goods worth about 24 dollars in seventeenth-century currency. In a letter written by Peter Schagehen on November 1626, the Dutch East India Company official reports back to the Netherlands that the Dutch "have purchased the Island Manhattes from the Indians for the value of 60 guilders." (The guilder was the Dutch currency until replaced by the Euro.) They named the city New Amsterdam.

The Dutch expanded their settlements for the next four decades. Meanwhile, Great Britain was busy colonizing its own territories in the Americas and had their eye on acquiring this valuable port city. They demanded the Dutch cede New Amsterdam to them in 1664. Dutch Director General Peter Stuyvesant wanted to resist, but he had little support. Stuyvesant and British Colonel Richard Nicolls reached an agreement that surrendered New Amsterdam to the British. The British renamed the island Manhattan.

Fast forward one century and New York found itself occupied by the British again during the American Revolutionary War before the colonies won independence and became the United States of America.

Fast forward two centuries and the separate cities of Manhattan, Brooklyn, Staten Island, the Bronx, and Queens voted to unite as one city in 1895. The decision took effect on January 1, 1898.

Waves of immigration significantly expanded and changed New York City, pumping the city full of new people, ideas, and cultures. Immigrants from Europe and Asia diversified the population, along with a significant African American population that migrated north to New York after the American Civil War.

Immigrating to New York was relatively easy before 1890. But the process became increasingly regulated with the establishment of Ellis Island in 1892 and the introduction of a quota system to regulate the nationalities of immigrants.

Immigrants over 16 years of age had to pass a literacy test in their native language beginning in 1917. The Immigration Act of 1924 instituted a quota system that favored European immigrants. The number of immigrants from any given country could not exceed 2 percent of the total number of people from that nation living in America according to the 1890 census. In other words, if there were 100 German people in the United States in 1890, only two German people could immigrate in 1924. Very few Chinese could immigrate to the United States due to the major restrictions posed by the Chinese Exclusion Act that stayed in effect from 1882 to 1943. Essentially, immigration reform made racism the law of the land.

The discriminatory quota system ended when Congress passed the Immigration and Nationality Act in 1965. Since then, immigration patterns have brought new waves of immigration from Latin America and Asia to New York City. In 2000, 36 percent of New York City's population was foreign born. Most of these 2.87 million people hailed from the Dominican Republic, China, Jamaica, Guyana, and Mexico. An estimated 800 languages are spoken in all five boroughs, and you can find just about every faith practiced.

This melting pot takes on a literal meaning when we're talking about the restaurant and bar scene. From Irish pubs to Chinese restaurants, the city's culinary scene reflects its rich history and diversity. So let's explore it by borough. First up, Manhattan.

MANHATTAN

BARBETTA

321 W 46TH ST, NEW YORK, NY 10036

(212) 246-9171 | BARBETTARESTAURANT.COM

For over a century, Barbetta has brought New York's theater district the finest in Italian cuisine and decor. Opened in 1906 by Sebastiano Maioglio, the restaurant has been run by his daughter Laura Maioglio for over five decades. The Maioglio family hails from the Piedmont region of Italy, which is home to some of Italy's finest wines and white truffles. The Maioglio family still owns property and operates a vineyard there. Since 1906, a piece of Piedmont can be found on Restaurant Row in Manhattan.

Stepping into Barbetta is like stepping into a museum. Antiques from the seventeenth and eighteenth centuries decorate the space: from bar stools so intricate you don't want to sit on them to the stunning chandelier previously owned by a royal family in Turin. But the restaurant was not always synonymous with luxury. Father and daughter had very different ideas about decor and price.

"My father's restaurant was not expensive," says Laura. "He didn't want it that way." Sebastiano opened Barbetta at age 26 on 39th street between 8th and 9th Avenues. He catered to a crowd that was more everyman than the upscale, older clientele you're now likely to see dining here before a Broadway show. In 1925, Sebastiano moved the operation seven blocks north to 46th street and into four nineteenth-century townhouses, where the operation has remained ever since.

Laura grew up in the brownstone apartment above Barbetta. Her parents exposed her to all sorts of art. Her childhood included frequent trips to museums, and at age six, she even attended her first opera. In high school she took a course in art history. "I wanted to learn more about the things I was seeing in New York," she explains. By seventeen, she had become an art

collector. At Bryn Mawr, she studied design and planned to be an architect. That changed when her father sold Barbetta.

Although she'd never been involved with running Barbetta, Laura did not want to see her father's restaurant transferred to someone else's hands. "I went to the purchaser, who I'd vaguely met, [and] I started to cry," recalls Laura. "I begged him to withdraw and he did." Laura's parents did not support her meddling, but she forged ahead anyway. It was 1962 and Laura was suddenly a restaurateur.

Laura funneled her knowledge of art history into redecorating and rebranding Barbetta. The result is a collector's paradise, albeit an expensive one. "People who came to the previous Barbetta are going to be shocked at the prices," she recalls thinking. The first floor includes a garden with a lovely fountain and a luxurious dining room featuring the aforementioned chandelier. "When I could use authentic pieces I did. When I could not, I had authentic pieces copied and shipped over [from Italy]," she explains. "I used to go to auctions a great deal," says Laura. "Every Saturday. That was my routine."

Pieces bought at auction also decorate the second floor, where Barbetta often hosts private functions. If you're not here for a private party, ask to look upstairs anyway, because it's very impressive. From matching gold-framed mirrors that look like they belong in Versailles to paintings that look like they belong in the Louvre, it's an artistic haven.

But it wasn't just the space that Laura infused with extra Italian flavor. She also made several additions to the menu. She imported wines from the family's Piedmont vineyard that had never been sold in America. The additions of Grignolino and Barbera signaled the beginning of a wine program that would grow to about 2,000 selections. In 1962, the kitchen began to churn out Piedmont specialties like risotto, wild porcini mushrooms, and polenta. Before gracing plates at Barbetta, these dishes had never been served in the United States.

The same year, Barbetta introduced American palates to white truffles. Extremely rare and thus extremely expensive, white truffles grow in Piedmont. The world's largest white truffle weighed in at just over four pounds and fetched over $60,000 at auction in 2014. Typically, humans use pigs to sniff out these special mushrooms that grow about ten inches underground. But Laura uses dogs known as truffle hounds.

On one occasion, Laura buried two pounds of white truffles worth $25,000 in Barbetta's garden. She intended to show guests what the truffle-hunting process looks like. She set one of her truffle hounds named Princess Diana loose to hunt the truffles down. But with ninety guests blocking the way, the dog's handler couldn't pull Princess Diana away before she ate a $300 truffle. The canine princess did not receive a bill.

So often, man has found a way around nature. But unlike other foods, a white truffle cannot be faked. Those in search of this "white gold" are truly at the mercy of Mother Nature and an animal's schnoz. The days of white truffles at Barbetta have passed. Laura's three truffle hounds have all passed away and she has no plans to get new ones. "We don't have clients who want to spend that kind of money [anymore]," she explains.

Laura makes frequent trips to Italy. "It's essential," she claims, not only for herself, but for her staff as well. During her father's reign, Italian immigration had a strong presence in New York. But nowadays, fewer Italians make America their destination. So Laura sends her cooks and chefs to Italy. She finds restaurants to host her employees for a few weeks so that they can learn and bring back new culinary skills to Barbetta.

The menu is Italian but does not offer standard dishes like spaghetti and meatballs or chicken parmigana. That's not fancy enough.

Main courses include the expertly prepared venison served alongside a unique pear croquette and soft, baked apple. And the Pacific wild swordfish is prepared in a delicious ragu combining lentils and balsamic vinaigrette. Barbetta features a plethora of risotto dishes all uniquely paired with items like roasted red beets or rosé champagne. Other main courses range from roasted rabbit in white wine–lemon sauce to linguine with pesto sauce. For dessert, the pastry chef presents the popular espresso chocolate cake, served with nuts and berries, alongside crème brûlée and panna cotta.

Several directors have chosen Barbetta's high-end setting as a backdrop for their film and television projects. Don Draper took a date to dinner at Barbetta on *Mad Men*. Woody Allen used Barbetta in his movies *Alice* and *Celebrity*, as did Martin Scorsese in *The Departed*. The restaurant's elegant atmosphere certainly lends itself to highly visual mediums and is practically an art piece itself.

So listen to a Baroque opera or throw on a frilly blouse and prepare yourself for an authentic northern Italian experience in New York City. Then head to Barbetta.

COTTON CLUB

656 W 125TH ST, NEW YORK, NY 10027

(212) 663-7980 | COTTONCLUB-NEWYORK.COM

"Hold it! Hold it all night! Hold it till next week!"

A trumpeter in the Cotton Club All Stars house band is holding a note on a Saturday night, his lungs in overdrive. He finally needs to inhale, and the note dissipates into thin air. The crowd claps in appreciation.

Here on 125th street in Harlem at the Cotton Club, this house band builds on the legacy of renowned African American performers like Lena Horne and Duke Ellington who performed for white audiences. Under the leadership of bootlegger and racketeer Owen ("Owney") Madden, this Harlem jazz club provided music and booze during Prohibition.

The club opened in 1920 at 142nd and Lennox under the management of World Heavyweight Boxing Champion Jack Johnson. But it didn't take off until 1922 when Owney Madden took over. Prohibition was the law of the land, and Madden was a troublemaker. The British-born gangster operated a brewery that pumped out 300,000 gallons of beer a day. His crew ran alcohol through New York and New Jersey. The New York Police Department even nicknamed him Clay Pigeon because he got shot so often. Madden decided to invest in the Cotton Club, where he could sell his alcohol stash for high prices. He actually purchased the club while in prison for manslaughter. After serving nine years out of a twenty-year sentence, he reentered society and set his sights on profits. To maximize his payoff, Madden decided to rebrand. Or, rather, discriminate.

Madden instituted a new policy: white customers only. Madden's discriminatory policy promoted African American music while making it exotic. White New Yorkers traveled uptown to experience music of "the other."

The club's decor even idealized slavery. The bandstand was decorated to look like a "big house" on a plantation and a painted backdrop included slave houses and cotton plants. Black performers often performed routines that stereotyped African Americans. Chorus girls had to be under 21 and light skinned. Even composers like W.C. Handy, known as the "father of the

blues," could not sit to hear their *own* music being performed. And emcees sometimes introduced Duke Ellington as a "master of jungle music."

The Cotton Club was one of many Harlem clubs that featured but simultaneously degraded performers. As Langston Hughes put it in *The Big Sea*, white people began "flooding the little cabarets and bars where formerly only colored people laughed and sang, and where now the strangers were given the best ringside tables to sit and stare at the Negro customers—like amusing animals in the zoo." But there were some clubs that functioned for and by black Americans, namely, the Renaissance Casino and Ballroom. The Renaissance even had its own basketball team that played in between musical sets and became a meeting place for the NAACP on occasion.

Still, the Cotton Club was an important place for musicians to develop their sound. Duke Ellington led the house band in 1927. Cab Calloway took over for him in 1931. Other performers included Louis Armstrong, Lena Horn, and Stepin Fetchit. The club gave many artists important career opportunities, while their whites-only customer rule reinforced their status as second-class citizens. As Duke Ellington crooned in his 1943 Carnegie Hall performance entitled "Black, Brown, and Beige":

> *And so, your song has stirred the souls / Of men in strange and distant places . . . / But did it ever speak to them / Of what you really are? . . . / How could they ever fail to hear / The hurt and pain and anguish / Of those who travel dark, lone ways / The soul in them to languish? / And was the picture true / Of you? The camera eye in focus . . . / Or was it all a sorry bit / Of ofay hocus-pocus?*

Had he been taken seriously? Or had he been seen as a bit of exotic magic, or "hocus pocus"?

The Cotton Club waned in popularity after the Harlem Riot of 1935. On March 19, 1935, 16-year-old Lino Rivera shoplifted a penknife from a dime store. The storeowner called the police. A crowd grew outside the store. Fearful the crowd would turn angry if the cops arrested the teenager, the shopkeeper decided not to press charges. But a rumor spread that the police had killed Lino. Thousands gathered to protest Lino's perceived murder. The protest turned violent. More than a hundred people sustained injuries and three died. About 200 stores suffered over $200 million in damages. The Cotton Club moved to midtown after the riot but closed in 1940.

John Beatty decided to resurrect the Cotton Club in 1978 in Harlem. For the last four decades, his modern incarnation of the club has operated at 125th and Riverside Drive. I was surprised that Beatty, despite having no affiliation with the original Cotton Club, could use the name and a similar logo. But, he reminded me, gangsters didn't exactly register trademarks. So the name was up for grabs. One crucial change differentiates the two Cotton Clubs: On a Saturday night in November the clientele is almost all African American.

Candles dance on small red cabaret tables throughout the intimate space. Funky mirrors reflect red hues from stage lights across the space. Pictures of the Cotton Club's many famous performers hang on its light purple walls. On especially busy nights, balcony seating provides a bird's eye view of the musicians seated on the grandstand.

The Cotton Club offers different programs every night. Mondays feature swing dancing and Fridays feature jazz and blues for $25 (not including food and drinks). Saturday and Sunday brunches pair with gospel for $43.50, and Saturday nights feature jazz with the Cotton Club All Stars house band and a buffet for $56 a person, not including drinks. The prices appear to attract a crowd that's decidedly older (around 40 plus) and elevate the evening to one that's a special night out. To attract a younger crowd, the Cotton Club has launched $20 jazz and blues Friday nights.

Tourists drive Beatty's business. On the night I enjoyed a performance, over half of the patrons left together on a bus. But perhaps the Cotton

Club's addition of cheaper Friday nights will attract more young, local music lovers to the venue.

The Saturday evening features about an hour of music from the band, during which patrons visit the buffet. Trumpet player Alvin Pazant has been the bandleader since the club re-opened under Beatty's management. A few singers join the band at the end of the night. A woman with a giant flower in her hair follows a young man who belts Marvin Gaye's "What's Going On?" She is Linda Hutchinson, also known as "Princess Billie." "She walked in one night . . . and asked could she perform after the show. I said 'Ok, let's put you up there, see what you can do,'" recalls Beatty. "She did OK." Fifteen years later, she's still a regular performer at the Cotton Club. She treats us to Louis Armstrong's "Sunny Side of the Street" and entices people to dance with a rendition of "The Electric Slide." She's followed by Danny Smalls, a two-decade-veteran of the Cotton Club. By 11:30 p.m., the evening of jazz and blues crescendos to a close.

The Cotton Club has a rich, problematic history. But today, it's doing what it was always meant to do: promote and incubate jazz for all.

DELMONICO'S

56 BEAVER ST, NEW YORK, NY 10004

(212) 509 -1144 | WWW.DELMONICOSRESTAURANTGROUP.COM

Before Delmonico's, there was no such thing as a restaurant in the United States. Well, not as we know the concept today. If you wanted a meal, you were at the mercy of whatever a chef had decided to prepare that day at an inn or tavern. Everyone got the same thing. Like your kindergarten teacher said: You get what you get, and you don't get upset.

But that started to change in France. After the monarchy fell at the end of the eighteenth century, royal cooks needed jobs. So they came up with a new concept: What if instead of making everyone eat the same thing, patrons could order anything they wanted à la carte? A dining revolution was afoot. And in 1837, that revolution spread across the Atlantic to the United States when Swiss brothers John and Peter Delmonico opened a fine dining establishment named Delmonico's. After fighting a revolution in the United States for the right to choose our representatives, Americans now had choice in the kitchen.

Both brothers had experience in the food industry. John had operated a wine shop and Peter had run a candy store. They decided to combine their efforts and move to the United States. They opened a cafe and pastry shop in 1827 called Delmonico & Brother. Three years later, they expanded their business to include a restaurant. John and Peter recruited their nephew Lorenzo to join them in New York in 1831. He became an integral part of their business.

The Delmonico brothers purchased a 220-acre farm on Long Island in 1834 where they grew vegetables for their enterprise. The same year, the brothers bought an apartment building. It's a good thing they did, because the next year, a fire completely destroyed their cafe and restaurant. But

with a second property already in their name, the brothers simply moved their cafe and restaurant operation to the boarding house for a year.

What had been a modest restaurant became a lavish, over-the-top fine-dining destination in 1837 when Delmonico's moved the restaurant into a new building at Beaver, William, and South William Streets. It was three-and-a-half stories tall with pillars imported from Pompeii and featured all-around glitz and glamour. Patrons named it The Citadel. It would dominate fine dining in New York for the next century.

The original menu included 12 soups, 32 hors d'oeuvres, 28 beef entrees, 46 veal entrees, 20 mutton entrees, 47 poultry entrees, 22 wild game entrees, 20 separately listed roasts, 46 seafood dishes, 41 vegetable and egg dishes, 19 pastries and cakes, 28 other desserts, 24 liqueurs, and 64 wines and champagnes.

Current owner Dennis Turcinovic wrote in an e-mail, "Delmonico's embraced change. The brothers were open to experimenting with new ideas, techniques, and concepts." Although others claim ownership, Delmonico's takes credit for the creation of three now-famous dishes: the Lobster Newberg, Eggs Benedict, and Baked Alaska. Turcinovic carries on that approach. "As much as we celebrate our culinary contributions, we are always striving to stay current and adopt recent trends."

Throughout the early twentieth century, Delmonico's opened several restaurants throughout Manhattan as the center of activity continued to shift uptown. Each of the restaurants was elegant, but if you wanted to turn up the swank-factor, you could pay for extra accessories. On one occasion, a guest arranged for everyone to sit on silk cushions embroidered with their names and to order from satin menus that had been hand-lettered in gold.

The nation's finest flocked to Delmonico's. Famous guests included writers Ralph Waldo Emerson and Charles Dickens. Many political figures visited the restaurant, including Ulysses S. Grant and Abraham Lincoln, who used Delmonico's at 14th and 5th Avenue for secret meetings with generals

during the American Civil War. Lincoln reportedly favored Delmonico's mashed potatoes topped with cheese and breadcrumbs. Napoleon once ate at Delmonico's, as did the inventor of the telegraph, Samuel F. B. Morse. President Andrew Johnson enjoyed a ten-course meal at Delmonico's in 1866 that included seven varieties of wine and ten sculpted pastries, one of which looked like the Washington Monument.

John Delmonico passed away in 1842, and Peter Delmonico retired in 1848. So in the second half of the nineteenth century, Lorenzo ran Delmonico's ventures by himself, quite successfully. By 1876, he had four restaurants and 400 employees. But things took a turn for the worse after Lorenzo died in 1881. No family heir could match the success that Lorenzo, Peter, and John had cultivated.

However, there were some bright spots after the original trio passed away. Delmonico's introduced Americans to avocados in 1895. (People nicknamed them "alligator pears.") And in 1902, by hosting a ladies luncheon, Delmonico's became the first establishment to allow women to dine without a male chaperone. But these bright spots could not outshine its troubles.

A Delmonico family feud hurt business and a changing America challenged the operation. Using wild game had become illegal, making certain Delmonico's dishes impossible. And duck had become less readily available, further impeding Delmonico's menu. More significantly, World War I cut into Delmonico's success. With tighter purse strings, middle class Americans opted for dance clubs and movie theaters instead of opulent dinners. In 1920, when Prohibition took effect, not only did Delmonico's lose alcohol sales, but its dishes that involved cooking with alcohol also disappeared or had to change. In 1921, police arrested a waiter and manager at Delmonico's for serving vodka and gin.

On May 2, 1923, *The New York Times* ran an embarrassing story about the once thriving family business: "Delmonico's $19,000 Rent Long Overdue." The next month, all of Delmonico's businesses closed. Owners auctioned off their assets. A restaurant that once defined luxury now earned *The New York Times* description of "dismantled and forlorn."

After the Delmonico family failed to keep their restaurant in business, other proprietors tried to cash in on the Delmonico name. In 1929, Oscar's Delmonico's opened at The Citadel. The Delmonico family opposed the unauthorized use of their family name, but a judge ruled that the name Delmonico had essentially become a part of the American vernacular, a term synonymous with high quality cuisine that belonged in the public domain. And so, Delmonico's has changed hands over the years, paying homage to the opulence and vision of the original owners.

Today, Dennis Turcinovic runs Delmonico's at 56 Beaver Street in the Financial District. His father purchased Delmonico's in 1998. Enter through

the circular columned entrance of the triangular building in business casual attire and prepare for a fine dining experience that strives to mimic the opulence of the original. Although I was expecting the restaurant to be larger and look more like a ballroom with high ceilings based on historical accounts, it is nonetheless an elegant set-up. The first floor features the main dining room, where white tablecloths and tiny lamps grace each table. Near the front of the dining room, a see-through cabinet displays vintage Delmonico's menus, including one that features "regular dinner" for 12 cents. Off the back wall, the first floor has a private boardroom. This square room contains a table that comfortably seats eight to twelve below a modern chandelier. Black and grey first-floor carpets conjure feelings of power and wealth, matching the black and white walls.

The menu's high prices make it the Ritz of the financial district. One of the hamburgers offered will set you back $38. But it's not just meat in a bun. This burger features bacon, truffle hollandaise, and an egg. The Prime New York Strip costs $49 and $58 gets you the 40-day dry aged Bone in Rib Eye. The dinner menu also features swordfish, lobster, chicken, and sides to share like ale-battered onion rings with buttermilk blue cheese dressing and a beets, cucumber, and feta combination in a pickled red onion and olive oil dressing. The restaurant's most popular dishes are the Delmonico's Steak, Billy's House Cured Bacon, and the Baked Alaska.

Turcinovic has expanded to a second location in midtown called Delmonico's Kitchen that offers a more casual atmosphere for slightly lower prices. For a taste of history, and to pay homage to the father of the American restaurant industry, head to Delmonico's.

EAR INN

326 SPRING ST, NEW YORK, NY 10013

(212) 226-9060 | EARINN.COM

Take a look at the famous painting, *Washington Crossing the Delaware*. Your eye is most likely drawn to Washington, standing center, looking stoically ahead toward freedom. Now look below Washington at the lone man of color rowing an oar. That's James Brown. Not James "Get Up Offa That Thing" Brown. This Brown served as General Washington's aide during the American Revolution. In the late eighteenth century, Brown built a home in Manhattan at 326 Spring Street, a stone's throw from the Hudson River. He opened a tobacco shop on the first floor and lived upstairs. Today, Brown's home operates as a neighborhood restaurant and bar, the Ear Inn.

His home became a brewery under Thomas Cooke, which catered to the neighborhood's many sailors whose ghosts reportedly haunt the joint today. Because New York City filled in plots of water nearby in 1825, Brown's house is now a couple blocks from the water, instead of a couple steps. In the early 1900s, the brewery added a restaurant. When Prohibition hit, it stayed in business as a speakeasy and brothel. After Prohibition, the hangout catered to an all-male clientele, where men could gamble, play pool, and trade stories. It had no name, and was known simply as "The Green Door" for its—you guessed it—green door. A simple neon sign lit up the letters "BAR" over the building.

New York City christened The Green Door a historic landmark in 1969. In 1973, Rip Hayman rented a room above the bar for a hundred dollars a month while studying at Columbia University. (Typing this sentence made me cry a little bit with envy.) Four years later, Hayman bought the building with some friends.

Hayman published a music magazine called *The Ear* at the time and decided to name his new bar after the journal. He needed the approval of the Landmark Commission to make changes. To avoid a long bureaucratic nightmare, Hayman found a loophole. He painted over part of the "B" in the "BAR" sign so that it looked like an "E." Now, the neon sign read "EAR" and the Ear Inn buzzed to life. Today, the sign shines day and night with the subtext, "Est. 1817 A.D." (I've come up empty in my search for eateries established B.C.)

Despite being a short walk from the Spring Street C/E subway station, the Ear Inn feels decidedly off the beaten path. Close to the water, it feels removed from the chaos of the city. Outside, two wooden tables artistically wrap around trees. A plaque on the ground reminds you this was once the beach: *"You are standing on the former Hudson River shore. The rocky beach was filled in for docks and landings for ships, which would off load goods onto this original wooden block sidewalk. Watch your step!"*

Inside the saloon there is a blend of maritime and music history. Rock and roll music plays overhead and nautical paintings and memorabilia grace the walls. Low ceilings and battleship grey paint even give the small space a ship's humble ambiance. White paper covers square and rectangular tables and crayons are provided for artistically inclined patrons, young or old.

The kitchen is best known for its burgers and they live up to the hype. The first bite sends juice oozing out from the generous patty. Without any condiments, the burger has enough flavor to satisfy and is so big that one tomato slice covers only about half the meat's surface area. The cowboy chili is piping hot with finely ground beef, beans, the slight crunch of onions, and cold sour cream that evens out the chili's temperature.

For a visit to the *other* James Brown's house, head west toward the water and pop into the Ear Inn.

FRAUNCES TAVERN

54 PEARL STREET, NEW YORK, NY 10004

(212) 968-1776 | WWW.FRAUNCESTAVERN.COM

If the walls at 54 Pearl Street could talk, they'd regale us with tales of colonial uprising, the early days of American government, bomb scares, and murder. For on this spot stands Fraunces Tavern, New York City's oldest and perhaps most storied tavern.

An American flag waves from the red brick building on the corner of Pearl and Broad in sight of the South Street Seaport. Water once sloshed in this spot in an area known as the "Great Dock." But in the 1680s, the city of New York filled in this and other plots to create land and generate income. The city sold 54 Pearl Street in 1686. The building erected on this plot housed a variety of businesses throughout the 1700s until Samuel Fraunces purchased the building in 1762 for 2,000 pounds. That year, he opened a tavern on the spot, naming it the Sign of Queen Charlotte, also known as the Queen's Head Tavern.

Fraunces hailed from the West Indies and came to New York in 1755. His nickname was "Black Sam," leading historians to question his ethnicity. The 1790 census lists Fraunces as "free, white, head of household" and portraits indicate a Caucasian complexion.

Fraunces's reputation as a gifted cook drove customers to the Queen's Head Tavern, where he offered items both savory and sweet. Despite naming his tavern for the queen of England, Fraunces sided with the Patriots, and his tavern became an important site for political developments in the American Revolution.

The Sons of Liberty gathered frequently at Fraunces Tavern. It was here that they devised the New York Tea Party of April in 1774. Playing second fiddle to Boston's Tea Party, the New York Tea Party took place aboard the British ship *The London* on April 22, 1774. The New York Sons of Liberty dumped tea from eighteen chests into the Hudson River and then used the empty chests to feed the flames of bonfires.

These young men "didn't have board meetings about planning a rebellion," says Jessica Phillips, executive director of the Fraunces Tavern Museum. Like Boston's Green Dragon Tavern, where the idea for the Boston Tea Party was born, Fraunces Tavern "was a gathering place for people to spread ideas."

Those ideas led to the outbreak of war and to the British occupation of New York City. "Some people equate the occupation of New York City to a team of locusts coming in and destroying the place," says Phillips. Food shortages were particularly problematic. Patriots resisted the British by failing to send goods into New York ports. But innocent civilians paid the price for this. The British held their prisoners in warehouses, churches, and on ships in the Hudson River. "More people died in those ships than on the battlefield," Phillips reveals. It's estimated that about 8,000 Patriots died in battle and about 11,000 in prison ships from disease, starvation, extremes of the weather, and mistreatment by the British.

A married father of seven, Samuel Fraunces left New York before the British took over. He escaped to his farm in Elizabeth, New Jersey, with his family in 1776. In his absence, his Loyalist son-in-law took over the tavern. Two years later, the British captured Fraunces in Elizabeth and forced him to work as a cook for General James Robertson. Fraunces used the opportunity to smuggle food, clothing, and money to Patriot prisoners. After the Revolution, Fraunces Tavern continued to serve as a focal meeting point and center of political activity.

On November 25, 1783, New York City celebrated Evacuation Day—the day the British occupation finally ended after seven years. New York's first American governor, George Clinton, hosted a celebration at Fraunces Tavern. New York would continue to celebrate Evacuation Day for roughly the next hundred years. But the holiday fizzled by World War I, when the United States was allied with the British.

Nine days later, George Washington held a dinner for his officers in the Long Room at Fraunces Tavern. It was a bittersweet affair. Washington was overjoyed that the British had left New York but was sad to say goodbye to his friends in attendance. As recorded in Colonel Benjamin Tallmadge's 1830 memoir, Washington said to those gathered, "With a heart full of love and gratitude I now take leave of you. I most devoutly wish that your latter days may be as prosperous and happy as your former ones have been glorious and honorable."

Tallmadge writes that Washington was "suffused in tears," but there is some scholarly disagreement over why. It is romantic to interpret

Washington's tears as a sentimental display of brotherly love for his officers, but they may have been tears of embarrassed shortcoming, as Washington had not secured the pensions his officers were promised by the Continental Congress. "Now that [the Revolutionary War] was over and victorious, people did need to get paid," explains Phillips.

But she's quick to point out that nobody really knows why Washington cried. One thing was for sure: The dinner was a way for the Continental Army's commander-in-chief to say, as Phillips puts it, "It's been an amazing journey, but I'm going back to my civilian life." George Washington journeyed from Fraunces Tavern to Annapolis to resign his command of the army before the Continental Congress at Maryland's State House on December 23, 1783. After a brief stint as a private citizen, he went on to become the nation's first president.

What is *not* disputed about Washington's last supper at Fraunces Tavern is how much he and his officers drank that night: a whopping 133 bottles of wine and a whole lot of punch and beer. Comedy Central's *Drunk History* may be closer to the truth than not: The average adult at the time drank four gallons of hard liquor and fourteen gallons of beer and cider a year. So much drinking led to many spills and breaks at Fraunces Tavern. In addition to paying for food and beverages, customers paid for the number of candles they used and any broken items. At one meeting of the New York Provincial Congress in 1776 at Fraunces Tavern, members broke sixteen wineglasses, six decanters, several tumblers, and a pudding dish.

According to a study published in 2014, American adults consumed an average of 556 drinks per year. If this seems high to you, fret not: The top 10 percent of drinkers account for over half of all alcohol consumption, majorly skewing averages. But before you accuse our founding fathers of being total drunkards, remember that they didn't drink water. "We think of alcohol differently than they would," explains Phillips.

Today, Fraunces Tavern is split into a museum upstairs that replicates the original tavern and a modern bar and restaurant downstairs. In addition

to The Long Room, the museum also includes the Clinton Room, named for New York Governor George Clinton. Much fancier than the Long Room's everyman wood and pewter, the Clinton Room radiates nineteenth-century luxury. The porcelain silverware and rug hail from China. The real star of the room is the wallpaper. Added in 1838, it was made in France by Jean Zuber et Cie. The company printed a picturesque background and allowed its customers to select the images in the foreground; in the Clinton Room the wallpaper depicts scenes from the British surrender at Yorktown and the British evacuation of New York.

For some blacks, coming to Fraunces Tavern meant learning their fate: freedom or slavery. About half a million blacks lived in the colonies when the American Revolution began, comprising approximately 20 percent of the total population. They fought for both sides of the conflict. At the beginning of the war, George Washington stated that no blacks could serve in the Continental Army. The decision submitted to the concerns of Southern slave owners who feared that arming their slaves would lead to uprisings. (Washington was a slave owner; at the time of his death, he owned 123 slaves.)

The British Army, however, recruited blacks to fight for the Loyalist cause. But don't start praising their moral superiority to young America just yet: In November 1775, Virginia's Royal Governor Lord Dunmore issued a proclamation promising freedom in exchange for military service to slaves of rebel owners, but *not* for slaves of Loyalists. The British wanted the extra manpower but also sought to weaken the rebels' economy. Taking away their slaves accomplished both.

As the Patriots saw blacks joining the Loyalist cause, they reversed their position at the start of 1777. So by the time the war concluded, about 5,000 blacks had fought in the Continental Army, with additional numbers fighting for the British.

After the war, victorious Americans demanded that the British return all stolen property. In slaveholders' eyes, that meant slaves that had been drafted into the British army. But the British wanted to keep their word: Freedom had been offered for fighting.

So before they left New York City, the British appointed General Samuel Birch to determine who had earned their freedom as Loyalist soldiers. He held what are known as "The Birch Trials" at Fraunces Tavern. To blacks who could prove their service to the British Empire with enlistment papers or a pay voucher, Samuel Birch granted Birch Certificates that gave them freedom and a ticket to Great Britain. Others opted for a trip to Canada. About 19,000 Loyalists (including 3,500 freed slaves) moved to British Territories in Canada. Ironically, some slaves who fought for American freedom were returned by Birch to their owners.

Fraunces Tavern also served as an important site of political activity in the new Republic. Samuel Fraunces found himself broke after the war. He wrote a letter to his friend George Washington asking to be paid for his service during the war. "George Washington wasn't able to give him money, but he was able to arrange leasing of government offices at Fraunces Tavern," says Phillips, providing a new way for Fraunces to fill his pockets. The young American government rented rooms at Fraunces Tavern for the Department of Foreign Affairs, the Department of War, and the Treasury in 1785.

Three months later, Fraunces sold the tavern to pursue other interests. An entrepreneur, he was "always looking for bigger and better things," says Phillips. A new owner purchased the tavern, and three years later, when the government departments terminated their leases, the tavern returned to its primary role as a place to eat, drink, and be merry.

From 1795 to 1800, the tavern operated as a boarding house under new owner Nicholas Romaine. In 1798, the tavern was the focus of a murder-suicide, when a man took his wife's life and then his own.

Throughout the 1800s, Fraunces Tavern continued to serve as a place of respite and spirits. Prominent guests in 1804 included Alexander Hamilton and Aaron Burr. The longtime political rivals visited Fraunces Tavern on July 4th for a meeting of the patriotic Society of the Cincinnati. A week later, Hamilton would die at Burr's hand. When Vice President Burr shot Hamilton in the stomach in a duel, or "affair of honor" in Weehawken, New Jersey, both New York and New Jersey charged Burr with murder, but he never faced punishment.

On the one-hundred-year anniversary of Washington's farewell dinner at Fraunces Tavern, a group of patriotic men formed the Sons of the Revolution in the State of New York (SRNY). John Austin Stevens spearheaded the group's formation when he found he was ineligible for membership in the Society of the Cincinnati. The nation's first patriotic club founded in 1783, the Society had strict membership rules: Only officers of the Continental Army and their French counterparts who served together for three or more years in the American Revolution and their first-born sons could become members. Stevens could not join, as his father was not the eldest

son of an original Society member. The Sons of the Revolution of New York opened membership to all male descendants of men who served in the military or with the federal or state governments during the American Revolution. They made it their mission to carry on the memory of those who achieved American independence, to celebrate important anniversaries in American history, and to spread the patriotic spirit generated by the country's forefathers.

To inaugurate the group, Stevens held a grand Turtle Soup Feast at Fraunces Tavern and was elected the group's president. (Note to political candidates: Forget the Super Pacs and try turtle soup.) The gigantic bowl that held the group's soup is on display at the Fraunces Tavern Museum. It's big enough to sit in. Evidently, our country has always had a problem with portion control. The SRNY purchased Fraunces Tavern in 1904 and continues to operate the site as a tavern and museum. In 1965, New York City declared Fraunces Tavern a city landmark.

Fraunces Tavern has survived two violent attacks since opening in 1762. In 1775, a British naval ship shot its cannons at the tavern, putting a hole in the roof. More recently in 1975, the Armed Forces of Puerto Rican National Liberation (FALN) left a briefcase containing roughly ten pounds of dynamite in Fraunces Tavern's entrance. It detonated, killing four and wounding fifty-three.

The dinner menu at the tavern features meat and seafood, from a classic 14-ounce Prime New York Strip or a 24-ounce Berkshire Pork Chop to a Wild Alaskan Salmon or Roasted American Red Snapper. I doubt our forefathers were as into kale as we are today, but for modern palates there's a baby kale Caesar salad with shallot rings, pecorino, and croutons on the menu. Vegetarians can enjoy the tavern's hand-made sweet corn and ricotta ravioli.

Lunch offers more casual fare, from Reubens and Turkey Burgers to a Crispy Chicken Biscuit or Berkshire Pork Belly served with avocado, cilantro, cheese, chickpeas, and a black bean spread.

The brunch menu features a $29 prix-fixe menu that includes an appetizer, main course, and either two mimosas or two Bloody Marys. Or go à la carte and choose from items like a watermelon slice seasoned with chili, lime, sugar, and salt, or the croissant French toast sweetened with berry compote and whipped cream.

Since 1762, Fraunces Tavern has been a place where people can eat, drink, and express their ideas. Says Phillips, "That's the freedom we fought for."

FRYING PAN

PIER 66 MARITIME IN HUDSON RIVER PARK, NEW YORK, NY 10011

(W 26TH STREET ENTRY)

(212) 989-6363 | FRYINGPAN.COM

The bike path along with West Side Highway has become a runner and cyclist's paradise. Beautiful grassy areas and piers provide picnic areas for lovers and room to play for canine friends. But it wasn't always so. Hudson River Park, which stretches five miles along the Hudson River from Battery Park up to 59th Street, was created in 1998 with the Hudson River Park Act. Before then, the sports complex Chelsea Piers provided the only known reason for New Yorkers to hike all the way west. John Krevey docked a retired lighthouse ship named the *Frying Pan* hidden behind Chelsea Piers. He turned the ship into a floating bar and restaurant in 1989. Under the radar for many years, the modest endeavor blossomed into one of the most popular destinations in New York and made going west a must.

A shoal shaped like a frying pan can be seen at low tide off the coast of Cape Fear in North Carolina. Known as the Frying Pan Shoal, this sand bar was so shallow that it caused many shipwrecks, earning its nickname as the "Graveyard of the Atlantic." The state placed a lighthouse here in an effort to ameliorate the situation, but it proved insufficient. So beginning in 1854, the state positioned a series of ships to act as lighthouses to warn approaching vessels. These floating lighthouses are called lightships and are named for the waters they guard. In 1929, the *Frying Pan* lightship floated into service.

The *Frying Pan*'s shape and size—133 feet long and 632 tons—enabled it to survive horrific storms. From 1929 to 1964, fifteen men aboard the *Frying Pan* protected the Frying Pan Shoals in good weather and bad. The lightship took a brief three-year break beginning in 1942 to guard the Panama Canal, but returned to North Carolina at the end of World War II.

But by the 1960s, the introduction of radar and global positioning systems made lightships obsolete and sent the *Frying Pan* into retirement in 1964. The lightship became a museum in Southport, North Carolina, before a private investor scooped it up with hopes of turning it into a floating restaurant. But, the project was abandoned, and so the *Frying Pan* remained docked at an oyster cannery on the Chesapeake Bay for a decade. The ship's neglect led to a broken pipe that caused the ship to sink. It remained underwater for three years. "Some say it was taking a nap before its next journey: New York City," says the ship's current owner Angela Krevey. Angela and her husband, John, bought the ship from a used car salesman and moved it to New York in 1989.

John hailed from Seattle, where the waterfront was king. He could not understand why New York's east and west waterfronts had yet to become a booming destination. With the purchase of the *Frying Pan*, John hoped to change that. He and Angela docked the *Frying Pan* behind Chelsea Piers and opened it as a restaurant. Restaurant may be a generous term, however. John's niece Danielle Kurtin, who runs the *Frying Pan* today, explains: "Thirteen years ago, I swear there were five tables." The *Frying Pan*'s clientele consisted mostly of people who wandered onto the ship. "[It was a] hidden treasure for some years," says Kurtin.

When Chelsea Pier extended to include a skateboard park and carousel, the *Frying Pan* had to relocate. But the move up to Pier 66 only helped business. With the addition of the bike path and the High Line—the park built on disused New York Central Railroad tracks along the Hudson—bringing lots of people to the water, the *Frying Pan* began to have greater visibility than ever before. "People wanted to come over here," says Kurtin. "It wasn't just a dirt yard anymore. If you make a park, people will come."

John expanded his business with several purchases. He bought a Lackawanna railroad barge on eBay and added a fireboat, the *John J. Harvey*, in 2000. This fireboat dates back to 1931. When it burst onto the scene at 20 miles an hour, it was the most powerful fireboat on the planet. On 9/11, the *John J.* came out of retirement to battle the flames at the World Trade Center and to evacuate Battery Park residents from Ground Zero. This floating trio comprises the *Frying Pan* mini-complex today.

The *Frying Pan* has come a long way since its humble beginnings. The kitchen once consisted of a grill fashioned from a large filled-in buoy. Today, that buoy has been converted into a flowerbed and replaced by a real kitchen that can feed the 6,000 to 9,000 patrons that come aboard on an average summer Saturday. The length of two football fields, it's a sprawling complex that never comes close to its capacity despite a high influx of patrons.

The kitchen stays true to its modest origins with casual items like hamburgers, hotdogs, and nachos. Patrons typically order at the kitchen kiosk

and then take their seats anywhere on the barge. But Kurtin is putting her degrees in architecture and design to use with plans to expand the *Frying Pan*'s offerings and aesthetic. "We're not just going to serve Pabst and nachos," she says. "We serve everything from hamburgers and hotdogs to lobsters." Indeed, the barge has a beer garden vibe, while the *Frying Pan* lightship offers a more upscale atmosphere with table service. But don't expect white tablecloths and violins. The patio furniture solidifies it as a casual spot, but the beautiful views of the Hudson and Freedom Tower elevate the environment, along with the light bulbs strung above umbrellas and canopies. At the helm, a large bell engraved "1929" rings to announce last call.

Below deck, the *Frying Pan* is a maze that features a dance floor and bar. It's grungy with very close quarters. Remember: This ship lived under water for three years! While the exterior has been restored, the interior retains its lived-in, barnacle-wall-paper aesthetic. It's a decidedly cool space to throw a private party or dance the night away. But even if there's a private event at the *Frying Pan*, part of the ship will always be open to the public. "We are part of the public environment," says Kurtin. Following in her uncle's footsteps, an early member of the Friends of Hudson River Park initiative, Kurtin believes that the *Frying Pan* is an accessible extension of the waterfront park.

Five years ago the *Frying Pan* was crowned the world's leading Corona seller. Read that again: The *world's* largest seller of Corona. And it's only open half the year! Now that the bar sells a wider selection of beers and has white wine sangria on tap, its Corona sales have dropped but are still exceptionally high, especially when you take its size into account. "We do volumes compared to Madison Square Garden and Yankee Stadium," reveals Kurtin. "Beer sales are through the roof." Those beers max out at 6 percent alcohol. "It's a moving barge," explains Kurtin. "[We have to] look out for everybody's safety." That's why you'll see ladders roped off and crewmembers' bedrooms locked up below deck. The *Frying Pan* wants you to have fun, but not *too* much fun.

For some G-rated entertainment, bring your kids to the *Frying Pan* on Sunday afternoons for arts and crafts inside the caboose that sits atop the railroad barge. You can grab a pitcher of sangria while your little ones craft boats or lobsters.

Luckily, the *Frying Pan* sustained minimal damage during Hurricane Sandy. The complex rises and falls with the tide. If there's ever another impending disaster, Kurtin's heading for the *Frying Pan*. "It's my Noah's Ark," she declares.

John Krevey passed away in 2011, but his hope to get people to the water has certainly survived. His niece has taken the wheel with boundless energy and vision to carry on John's nautical legacy. For stunning views, refreshing drinks, and a slice of history, head west to the *Frying Pan*.

GRAND CENTRAL OYSTER BAR & RESTAURANT

GRAND CENTRAL TERMINAL

89 E 42ND STREET, NEW YORK, NY 10017

(212) 490-6650 | OYSTERBARNY.COM

To find the best fish, sometimes you have to go underground. That's the philosophy of the Grand Central Oyster Bar & Restaurant, a seafood restaurant located on the lower level of the world's largest train station. The Oyster Bar has been attracting fish lovers with its famous vaulted ceilings and fresh fish since the terminal opened in 1913. Shucking five million oysters a year, the Oyster Bar has become an important part of Grand Central's history.

After ten years of construction, 30,000 tons of steel, and $80 million in costs—$2 billion in today's dollars—Grand Central Terminal opened on

February 2, 1913. Stretching 69.8 acres, it was and remains the largest train station in the world. Builder Cornelius Vanderbilt designed the station, incorporating acorns and oak leaves into the design as references to the Vanderbilt family crest. Vanderbilt designed a station with few stairs, opting for ramps modeled after the slopes that led to Julius Caesar's Roman army camps.

Fifteen thousand visitors poured into the terminal on the first day it opened. They took in the grandeur of its design, marveling at its ceiling painted with 2,500 stars for the zodiac sky in the Mediterranean in March. The ceiling at Grand Central is one of the artistic wonders of New York City, so take a moment to stop moving and crane your neck to look at it. Then, take the ramps down to the lowest level of the terminal to enter the Grand Central Oyster Bar & Restaurant, and be amazed by the architectural elements designed by Spanish architect Rafael Guastavino.

Guastavino designed the restaurant's five vaults and a herringbone pattern of rectangular terra cotta ceiling tiles. Patented in 1885 as his "Tile Arch System," Guastavino's tiled vaults helped to create a unique space that continues to delight. The lights hugging each curve give the space a bright, welcoming feel despite its underground location. Guastavino's other credits are many and include the Boston Public Library, the Great Hall at Ellis Island, the vaulted arcade under the Queensborough Bridge, the Elephant House at the Bronx Zoo, and dozens more in New York City and other American cities.

In the early twentieth century, long-distance train travel had a romantic quality to it. Fast food was still a few decades away, so travelers dressed up and ate under chandeliers at the Oyster Bar before embarking on their travels. But it wasn't just travelers who dined at the restaurant. The Oyster Bar also attracted high society.

Grand Central went into a decline in the mid-twentieth century as more New Yorkers opted for travel by plane or car, and some city dwellers left for the suburbs. By the 1970s, Grand Central became a place to buy drugs or prostitutes and shelter the homeless. This climate sent the Oyster Bar

& Restaurant into bankruptcy in 1972. But the Metropolitan Transportation Authority breathed new life into the institution when it asked New York restaurateur Jerome Brody to revive the iconic restaurant in 1974. Brody had made his mark on the New York City restaurant scene with some of New York's great restaurants including The Four Seasons, The Rainbow Room, and Gallagher's, among others.

When Brody visited the restaurant it was literally caked with grime. The famous terra cotta tiles had turned black. "I was horrified," recalls Jerome's wife, Marlene Brody. "I thought, this is something that he's embarking on that's going to be extremely difficult." But Brody accepted the challenge. He polished the restaurant's design, creating five distinct seating areas, each with its own vibe and character: the counters, the oyster bar, the lounge, the saloon, and the dining room.

The lounge, a small open area containing striking white tulip tables and wraparound booths is the first section you'll see upon entering. It has a 1960s retro feel and, except for the "No Smoking" sign, Don Draper and his *Mad Men* colleagues would feel right at home here. In fact, Draper and Roger Sterling have oysters and martinis in the lounge in season one of the AMC hit. The Lounge is a great place to wait for your date or enjoy a cocktail from the bar.

Just past a lobster tank to the left of the lounge is the dining room. Red-and-white-checkered tablecloths are draped over square tables accommodating two or four diners in the spacious area, which can seat 280 customers.

To the right of the lounge are three U-shaped counters and the oyster bar. The white Formica counters are communal eating areas and their U-shape prompts conversation among patrons seated together. The oyster bar offers additional entertainment: a front row seat to the restaurant's shucking station. A wooden board above the bar lists the day's selection of oysters, clams, shrimp, lobster, scallops, and more from all over the map. Written by hand in black marker on rectangular panels, they look like the leader boards used in golf tournaments. On a Monday afternoon in autumn, the restaurant had items on ice from Long Island, New Zealand, Maine, Rhode Island, Washington State, Massachusetts, Mexico, and New Jersey.

Tucked away through swinging half-doors is the saloon, a room for decidedly upscale cowboys. With lower ceilings and softer lighting, it's a quieter and more intimate space. Paintings of ships decorate the walls, along with a few encased ship models, creating an environment for captains of industry to do business over lunch or dinner.

Brody wanted to make the Oyster Bar an excellent seafood restaurant. When it first opened it had, of course, served oysters, but served a full range of products in addition to seafood. Until 1927, when the last oyster beds in New York City were shut down due to toxicity. Oysters were very, very plentiful in New York," says Marlene. "[The] streets were filled with oyster shells."

Jerome wanted to expand the restaurant's seafood offerings. "We went to every fish restaurant within a radius of fifty miles. The fish really wasn't that good. We had an opportunity."

Brody hired George Morfogen as the restaurant's fish buyer. Each morning, Morfogen selecting thousands of pounds of fish for the Oyster Bar. Brody also sought to establish the Oyster Bar as a great place for wine enthusiasts. He sent General Manager Mario Staub across the country to tour California vineyards. Brody's focus on wine paid off. In 1996, the restaurant won the Award of Excellence from *The Wine Spectator*.

During Brody's tenure at the Oyster Bar, Grand Central Terminal faced a serious threat. Pennsylvania Central Railroad, the group that owned Grand Central, planned to build a tall office building on top of the terminal. "We just thought it was an abomination," says Marlene. "You know what happened

to Penn Station." The original Beaux-Arts-style Pennsylvania Station, completed in 1910 and considered one of New York's architectural jewels, was demolished in 1963 and replaced by an unattractive eyesore that frustrates New Yorkers today. Many feared that Grand Central would face the same fate.

In January 1975, a judge invalidated Grand Central's designation as an official historical landmark, which left it vulnerable to Penn Central's plans for change. So the Municipal Arts Society's Committee to Save Grand Central Station formed to put political pressure on City Hall. The most prominent member of the committee—Former First Lady Jackie Kennedy Onassis. She joined the director of the Met, the Manhattan borough president, and the president of the Museum of the City of New York. The committee held a press conference at the Grand Central Oyster Bar on January 30, 1975. To a throng of reporters, architect Philip Johnson argued, "Europe has its cathedrals and we have Grand Central. Europe wouldn't put a tower on a cathedral." Mrs. Onassis said, "I think if there is a great effort, even if it's at the 11th hour, you can succeed, and I think and I know that's what we'll do."

In a letter to New York Mayor Beame, she elaborated: "Is it not cruel to let our city die by degrees, stripped of all her proud moments, until there is nothing left of all her history and beauty to inspire our children? If they are not inspired by the past of our city, where will they find the strength to fight for her future?"

Mrs. Onassis's involvement pushed the local story into the national spotlight. The committee took their appeal to reinstate landmark preservation status to the U.S. Supreme Court, which upheld the designation in 1978, ensuring no structure could be built atop the station. Today Grand Central Terminal remains an architectural beauty.

In 1990, Executive Chef Sandy Ingber joined the Oyster Bar as the new fish buyer. He begins each day in the Bronx at the Fulton Fish Market. By 4:30 a.m., Ingber has selected the fish to be served that day at the Oyster Bar. At 6:00 a.m., he reports to the restaurant, where his standing orders of oysters from at least ten different states have arrived. "It's a showcase for

small oyster farmers," says Ingber. "It's always been one of my joys . . . to give the small guy a place to showcase his oysters."

Predictably, oysters are the Oyster Bar's top seller. The restaurant sells "well over a million oysters a year," according to Ingber. That's about 4,000 to 5,000 oysters-on-the-half-shell sold per day, and does not include oysters used in other dishes. Clam chowder—New England and Manhattan— takes second place at the cash register as the restaurant sells between 400 and 500 bowls a day.

The Oyster Bar & Restaurant hosts a number of festivals each year. In June, the Herring Festival celebrates the first herring of the season shipped from Holland. Officials from the Dutch embassy come to the Oyster Bar for the festival, enjoying herring served from a Dutch street cart. Each September, the Oyster Bar & Restaurant hosts Oyster Frenzy. The event features an oyster-shucking competition, chef demonstrations, an oyster-slurping contest, free bloody Mary oyster shooters, and live music.

Marlene oversees all franchising of the Oyster Bar. There are two additional Oyster Bar restaurants in Brooklyn and Tokyo. Over the clinking of silverware and the slurping of oysters, you're sure to overhear conversations in several languages at the Grand Central Oyster Bar. The restaurant attracts many tourists, but also generations of families returning to the restaurant as loyal customers. Ingber says it's common to see customers at the Oyster Bar dining with a grandparent who instructs, "You gotta have an oyster stew like I did . . . " For generations, seafood lovers and weary travelers have indeed gone underground to find the freshest fish.

JULIUS

159 WEST 10TH STREET, NEW YORK, NY 10014

(877) 746-0528 | WWW.JULIUSBARNY.COM

AND

THE STONEWALL INN

53 CHRISTOPHER STREET, NEW YORK, NY 10014

(212) 488-2705 | WWW.THESTONEWALLINNNYC.COM

We, the people, declare today that the most evident
of truths—that all of us are created equal—is the star
that guides us still, just as it guided our forebears
through Seneca Falls, and Selma, and Stonewall . . .
—*Barack Obama, Inaugural Address, January 21, 2013*

Seneca Falls was a place of importance for women's rights, Selma for African American rights, and The Stonewall Inn for gay rights. A riot at the Mafia-run Stonewall Inn in June 1969 catalyzed the gay rights movement in the United States, and continues to be an important spot for supporters of LGBT equality. But long before The Stonewall, gay men gathered at the city's oldest gay bar, Julius. It was here that four men staged a "sip in" to protest the city's discriminatory laws against homosexuals.

Standing on the corner of 10th street and Waverly Place, Julius has been serving drinks since 1864. The structure dates back to an 1840 grocery store, and it operated as a speakeasy during Prohibition. It attracted many jazz and literary figures before morphing into a betting bar. Kentucky Derby pictures above the bar honor this past, and when current owner Helen Buford opened the safe one day she found old betting sheets. "Legal or not, it was something they did," she says. As Greenwich Village became

the place to go if you were gay in New York, Julius morphed into a gay bar by the 1950s.

A decade later, gay sex had become legal in *one* state. Illinois legalized sodomy in 1962. Sodomy laws would not be repealed in California until 1976 and in New York, not until 1981. During the Cold War, the U.S. government believed that the Soviets recruited disenfranchised Americans to work as spies. So targeting homosexuals was not only a matter of moral urgency, but potentially of political urgency, as well. Or so they reasoned.

Identifying as homosexual was not technically illegal, but engaging in homosexual acts or public displays of gayness (PDG) could be classified as "disorderly conduct," according to New York's law. Being openly gay could result in the loss of a job or one's home. If an individual was not wearing at least three items of gender-appropriate clothing, that warranted arrest. The plain-clothes police were known to entrap homosexuals, so precautions were taken. Patrons at Julius, for instance, drank facing the bar. If they angled their bodies outward toward the space, this could be interpreted as "solicitation." And if a bar propagated homosexual activity, it could be swiftly shut down. That is, if the owners managed to even *get* a liquor license.

The New York State Liquor Authority (SLA) did not grant liquor licenses to businesses that "suffer or permit [their] premises to become disorderly." But they wouldn't define disorderly. They wanted to leave it open to interpretation—*their* interpretation. When the SLA shut down Gloria's Bar & Grill in 1939, they characterized the bar as a gathering place for "undesirable people" and called the manager "a fag and leader of that element." With the SLA in New York and analogous agencies in other states, operating a gay bar or allowing PDG at "straight bars" came with a serious threat of closure. To the average barkeep, the risks were too great.

Enter: The Mafia. With the money to pay the cops to look the other way, the Mafia could operate gay bars and turn a profit by overcharging customers. Helen Buford suspects that Julius had Mafia ties. The Stonewall Inn, on the other hand, had *very clear* ties to the Mob.

Tony "Fat Tony" Lauria bought The Stonewall in 1966, but he answered to Matthew "Matty the Horse" Ianniello. The space dated back to the 1840s, when it functioned as a stable, and then housed a succession of businesses. Fat Tony renovated the restaurant that had been in the space and reopened it as a gay club in 1967, or, a private "bottle service" club. Private clubs did not need liquor licenses since they were BYOB. Loophole? Check. Customers signed their names into a guest book upon entry to uphold the membership technicality but knew to sign in with a pseudonym.

Although operating outside the law was a victory for equal rights, it was a major loss for hygiene. Without anyone to answer to but themselves, the Mafia did not make cleanliness and safety their priorities. The Stonewall had only one exit. Toilets overflowed. And there was no running water behind the bar. So bartenders routinely sold drinks in dirty glasses. But the Mafia made water an important ingredient *before* drinks got to the bar by watering down the supply. This made their alcohol inventory last longer. They also overcharged for drinks.

The Mafia employed vertical integration—controlling all aspects of a business and cutting out a middleman. They controlled alcohol distribution and the sources where it would be poured. In addition to The Stonewall, Ianniello owned other gay bars—The Hay Market, the Peppermint Lounge, and cross-dresser bar Gilded Grape.

While things weren't perfectly clean or safe at The Stonewall, the bar was an important part of gay culture in New York City. It was also "home" to some of New York's homeless LGBT youth. After their families kicked them out, some young gay men and women used The Stonewall not only for camaraderie, but also for shelter from the hot summer sun or the harsh winter cold. Inside, they danced to rock and roll or soul playing from the jukebox. The Mafia didn't make much money off these kids and their three-dollar admission price. But they did rake in considerable dough by blackmailing famous, closeted homosexuals. Pay up, or be outed.

Although the Mafia bribed the Sixth Precinct police $1,200 a month to look the other way, police still raided The Stonewall about once a month. But Mafia-run businesses knew how to prepare. They usually kept the bulk of inventory away from the property, so that even if police confiscated all the alcohol on the premises, they didn't lose too much product. Before opening, Fat Tony also had steel doors with multiple locks installed to impede swift police entry in the event of a raid. He also ordered the windows be reinforced with plywood to keep police from breaking them to gain entry. Plus, corrupt cops sometimes tipped Mafia-run businesses off before a raid so they could prepare.

The LGBT community routinely faced resistance from politicians campaigning for election. These political hopefuls led cleanup efforts that included identifying and closing gay bars. In particular, Mayor Robert Wagner closed practically all of New York's gay bars in advance of the 1964 world's fair. But many gay bars reopened after the fair closed, including The Stonewall.

Hostile conditions had begun to push LGBT men and women to their breaking points. The tide was turning toward revolution. The first official gay rights organization, The Mattachine Society, formed in 1950 in Los Angeles and then opened a New York branch in 1955. The name "Mattachine" comes from Italian jesters in the 1500s known to tell the truth in the face of everyone else's dishonesty. While African Americans staged sit-ins across the country to fight for racial equality, the Mattachine Society staged a "sip-in" at Julius.

Four young men led by Mattachine President Dick Liestch went in search of a bar that would not serve them with the intention of suing. They planned to enter, to announce their status as homosexual men, to pledge to remain orderly, to be refused service, and to sue the pants off the State Liquor Authority.

With reporters in tow, it took them a few tries to be denied. They intended to stage the sip-in at Ukrainian-American Village Restaurant, which bore a sign that said "If You Are Gay, Please Go Away." But by the time they got there, it was closed. They tried two more bars—Howard Johnson's Restaurant and The Waikiki—but received service at both. They decided to try Julius next. Police had raided Julius just ten days earlier. Even though it was a gay bar, the men knew that if they blatantly stated they were homosexual, the bartender would refuse to serve them. The bar's license was on the line, after all.

And so, on April 21, 1966, the men of the Mattachine Society entered Julius, announced their status as gay men, and were promptly refused service. They got the photo op they wanted. The bartender, who was certainly on their side, placed his hand over a glass in a display of discrimination. In today's world, this is the type of photo that would have gone viral in hours. The photo did the trick.

The Mattachine Society took the SLA to court and won. No laws actually changed, but New York City's Commission on Human Rights did declare that gay people could not be refused service and the Sip-In energized a growing movement to fight back against discrimination.

In the 1960s, the Public Morals division of the New York Police Department was after homosexuals and the Mafia. Raiding gay bars could take out both. In 1969, this division suspected the Mafia of blackmailing gay men in the financial industry, then using their leverage to get the men to trade stolen securities in Europe. By closing gay clubs, the division could check their hypothesis by tracing the bonds in play. In the last three weeks of June, Detective Charles Smythe and Deputy Inspector Seymour Pine raided five Greenwich Village gay bars. They seized alcohol and arrested employees at The Stonewall on June 24, 1969. But The Stonewall Inn was open for business the next day. Annoyed that their raid had proven so insignificant, Smythe and Pine planned another raid for June 28. This raid would have major significance.

Eight plain-clothes police officers entered The Stonewall Inn on Saturday, June 28, 1969, at 1:20 a.m. Deputy Inspector Pine led the group with a search warrant for the suspicion of illegal alcohol sales at the bar. The officers confiscated cases of liquor and demanded identification from the approximately 200 people inside. Patrons dressed in women's clothing were asked to enter the women's restroom to prove their sex. After their IDs were checked, non-cross-dressers were dismissed. But instead of dispersing, they remained outside The Stonewall. A large crowd formed and began to chant "Gay power!" and to sing "We Shall Overcome."

The police arrested thirteen people for harassment, resisting arrest, and disorderly conduct toward police vehicles. One woman in handcuffs tussled with police while complaining that her cuffs were too tight. The officer hit

her on the head with a billy club. She yelled to the crowd, "Why don't you guys do something!?" This was the straw that broke the camel's back. The crowd launched into full-blown resistance.

They threw coins, bottles, cobblestones, and beer cans, set small fires in garbage cans, and attempted to break into The Stonewall, where officers had barricaded themselves. The throng of protestors doubled in size to about 400 that night. Riots continued for about three hours. Four officers sustained injuries, including one broken wrist.

The next day, The Stonewall opened for business and gave away free soft drinks. That night, about 2,000 protestors gathered for another night of rioting. They set more trashcans on fire and attacked police cars.

Sunday was mostly quiet, in part thanks to the Mattachine Society, who met with the mayor and police and posted a sign encouraging angry LGBT supporters to embrace peace. They posted a sign in The Stonewall's front window that said: "WE HOMOSEXUALS PLEAD WITH OUR PEOPLE TO PLEASE HELP MAINTAIN PEACE AND QUIET CONDUCT ON THE STREETS OF THE VILLAGE."

Headlines seemed to side with the police. Most offensive was the *New York Daily News*, which ran a piece on July 6, 1969, with the headline, "Homo Nest Raided, Queen Bees Are Stinging Mad," in which the author compared patrons of The Stonewall to the freaks of *Alice in Wonderland* and described The Stonewall as a "mecca for the homosexual element who wanted nothing but a private little place where they could congregate, dance, and do whatever little girls do when they get together." This article hangs framed in The Stonewall today.

The Village Voice ran a piece by Lucian Tuscott that incited 500 to riot outside its headquarters on Wednesday around 10:00 p.m. Tuscott referred to protestors as "the forces of faggotry" and used the words "fag" and "dyke" to describe particular subjects in his article. Although Tuscott's article included quotes from protestors who used the fa-word to describe themselves (i.e. people chanting, "I'm a faggot! And I'm proud of it!" and an interaction with gay writer Alan Ginsberg in which he said, "Defend the fairies!"), Tuscott's use of the word outraged many. In the same way the n-word has been re-appropriated by the black community, the fa-word was for gays only and not for the use of reporters. So outside the newspaper's offices gathered not only LGBT supporters, but also members of the Black Panthers and the Yippies (Youth International Party). For about an hour, they scuffled with police and looted nearby businesses, resulting in several injuries.

The New York Times ran a piece the morning after the riots, "4 Policemen Hurt in 'Village' Raid: Melee Near Sheridan Square Follows Action at Bar." The headline immediately placed sympathy with the police, rather than the customers at The Stonewall.

On the first anniversary of the Stonewall Riots the first Gay Pride Parade was held. It started in Sheridan Square and marched up Sixth Avenue to Central Park for a "gay-in." The parade continued to grow and is now an annual event.

In 1973, as part of an effort to repair and improve conditions between police and homosexuals, the NYPD's Sixth Precinct challenged the Mattachine Society's baseball team to a friendly game. The police beat the New York Matts 15-0, but it was a victory for both sides. Among the police players was Frank Toscano, who'd been present at the Stonewall Riots. He told *The New York Times*, he "knew right then, or the day after [the riots], that there had to be a better way." Baseball was a start.

Although The Stonewall operates today, it closed for many years. After the riots, gay groups decided to boycott Mafia-run businesses, for although they'd made gay congregation possible, they'd done so under unsafe and unfair conditions. The Stonewall tried to stay in business as a juice bar, but that didn't pay the bills. It closed three months after the riots. Various stores leased the space for the next two decades. The Stonewall tried to make a comeback in 1987, but closed once again. In 1993, a third incarnation of The Stonewall opened and has remained.

In 1999, The Stonewall Inn earned a spot on the National Register of Historic Places. And in 2015, the bar became a New York City Landmark. It was the first time LGBT history was used to establish landmark status in the Big Apple. In its decision, the Landmarks Preservation Commission wrote: "The Stonewall Inn has a special character and a special historical and aesthetic interest and value as part of the development, heritage, and culture characteristics of New York City."

Helen Buford and her husband took the reins of Julius. They were not actively seeking a gay bar, but Buford feels a personal connection to what Julius stands for. "I never fit in with everybody else," she reflects. "I can understand the struggle of . . . not doing everything that you're supposed to do." Although she didn't experience the same persecution that LGBT men and women faced, "Marrying out of my race, I experienced that struggle in a different way," she comments.

"We all love this woman," a regular tells me one afternoon. It's mutual. Buford solicits opinions and ideas from her regulars. Their comfort is a major priority. "After all, this is their living room," she states.

When a hate crime took place at Julius in 2010, Buford worked to make sure it never happened again. She met with Christine Quinn, the first openly gay City Council Speaker, and the police, after which she made a few changes. Up until that point, Julius only had someone working the door at night. So Buford added a daytime door attendant. "As long as people are respectful of the place, they are welcome. Once they are not, they are not welcome," says Buford. "We haven't had a problem since."

Once a month, Julius holds a dance party in honor of the now-defunct Mattachine Society. Actor/writer/director John Cameron Mitchell (*Hedwig and the Angry Inch, Rabbit Hole*) hosts the parties with Amber Martin on the third Thursday of the month.

On June 27, 2015, the front page of *The New York Times* featured the headline "Equal Dignity: 5-4 Ruling Makes Same-Sex Marriage a Right Nationwide" above twelve pictures of same-sex couples embracing or kissing. When the Supreme Court made that historic ruling, Julius and The Stonewall Inn once again became focal points for New York's supporters of LGBT rights. Crowds gathered to celebrate at both locations. One of those celebrating at Julius was Brendan Byrnes. A few years earlier, Byrnes wed his longtime-partner Stephen Cabral at Julius: "When we first moved [to

New York] we sort of knew the historical significance of Julius," he recalls. "We would go once in a while." When New York legalized same-sex marriage in 2011, Brendan says he and Stephen knew The Stonewall would be a madhouse, so they decided to visit the lesser-known Julius. "[We] started to talk about the possibility of us getting married," remembers Brendan. They loved the history of the sip-in and thought Julius would be a "really fun place to get married."

And so, on December 2, 2014, on the twenty-fifth anniversary of their first date, Byrnes and Cabral tied the knot at Julius. Buford borrowed a small stage from The Stonewall—"there's no rivalry of any sort," she says— and the couple said "I do" on a normal day of operation feted by family, friends, and random customers. For four hours, Byrnes and Cabral covered the whole bar's tab as they celebrated their nuptials. "It was the most loving, sincere wedding I have ever been to," says Buford. "[We're] still making history," she adds proudly.

Ironically, as the nation has become a more equal place for LGBT individuals, gay bars have gone into decline. One explanation is financial: Bigger businesses push the little guys out. Another theory says that without the stigma of being LGBT, individuals no longer feel the need to self-segregate in an LGBT environment for their comfort or safety. But Buford believes that there will always be a need for gay bars. "The bars do need to stay," she says. "You can still come here and safely grab your partner and hug them and kiss them without anybody taking a second look. Just because everything is legal does not change everybody's minds."

So much had changed since rioters fought back against police harassment and unfair laws five decades ago. Both Julius and The Stonewall Inn prove that revolution truly can begin in a bar.

KEENS STEAKHOUSE

72 W 36TH STREET, NEW YORK, NY 10018

(212) 947-3636 | WWW.KEENS.COM

Smoking is so last century. And at one time, the place to do it was Keens. Opened in 1885 as a gentlemen's smoking club, Keens evolved into one of the city's foremost chophouses and continues to be the city's leading destination for lamb chops.

In the late nineteenth century, Herald Square served as New York's theater district. The Lambs Club was one theater group contributing to the arts scene. They established their headquarters next door to the Garrick Theater, where their manager, Albert Keens, decided to open a restaurant, saloon, and smoking room. Patrons paid five dollars a year to store their fragile churchwarden pipes on the premises. More than a century later, the tradition endures at Keens Steakhouse.

Keens boasts the world's largest collection of churchwarden pipes, tallying 90,000. These pipes are very long, usually stretching about fifteen inches. They hail from early eighteenth- and nineteenth-century Europe and got their name because churchwardens, who kept watch over churches at night in a time when church doors were never locked, smoked to pass the time during the night shift. The long stem of the pipe kept smoke and the pipe from obstructing the line of vision of the watchman, so he could do his job properly. Necessity truly is the mother of invention.

"The pipe club was active until 1978," says James Conley, Keens's service director, who doubles as the house historian. Members stored their pipes at Keens, thousands of which are currently mounted on the ceiling in no particular order. Prominent members like Teddy Roosevelt, Babe Ruth, Buffalo Bill, and John Barrymore smoked at Keens. In more recent years, celebrities from Jerry Stiller and Liza Minnelli to Chuck Norris and Arthur

Ashe received honorary membership. When a member of the club dies, someone at Keens ceremoniously breaks his or her pipe so that it can never be used again.

Mayor Michael Bloomberg was inducted into Keens's pipe club, ironically, the day before his citywide smoking ban took effect in 2003. Bloomberg happened to be dining at Keens on the eve of the ban and the restaurant presented him with his own pipe. Before the ban, "our bar was thick with smoke," says Conley, who has been with Keens since 1999. But the ban came at a good time. People were smoking less, but eating more meat. "The Atkins diet became an important diet," says Conley. "A lot of people thought they had to have a diet based on meat. That brought a whole new wave of clientele."

After 9/11, Keens also found more patrons coming through the doors seeking a connection to old New York. "People wanted to grab on to something that had been here a long time," says General Manager Bonnie Jenkins. "[That] introduced Keens to younger people." Traditionally having catered to "the man in the gray flannel suit" as Conley puts it, younger diners made for some comical interactions. "The other day someone asked me for a fireball [shot]," says Bonnie. "I said, 'We're not groovy like that.'"

For so long, Keens really was "men, men, only men," as Jenkins puts it. All that changed when actress Lillie Langtry sued Keens after the all-male club refused to serve her in 1905. She won the gender discrimination suit, paving the way for women not only to dine at Keens, but to become members of the pipe club as well. Keens held a dinner honoring Langtry in 1906 and named a room for her upstairs. "Certainly by the forties and fifties, from what we can see from photographs, there were lots of women here," says Conley. When I visited Keens on a weekday at lunch hour, men filled about two-thirds of the seats. "Yes, male clientele is the predominant clientele," Jenkins asserts, but Keens "definitely appeals to women, families, [and] corporate outings," she adds.

Keens became a popular destination for artistic folks in its early years, from writers and publishers to actors who snuck in for a drink wearing full makeup during their intermissions at the Garrick Theater. The establishment's theatrical roots have inspired the decor, which features a plethora

of artistic memorabilia including one particularly impressive item: the playbill Lincoln was holding when he died at Ford's Theatre on April 14, 1865. The *Our American Cousin* playbill hangs in a room named for Lincoln. "That became the starting point of a big collection," says Conley. Indeed, the Lincoln Room is teeming with all things Lincoln, including a handwritten copy of the "Gettysburg Address" (albeit not authenticated).

The Lambs Room celebrates all things theatrical, including a bevy of portraits of actors from the 1800s. "People that are theater buffs will come here and make all kinds of discoveries," says Conley. The centerpiece of the room is a giant painting of a tiger by Alexander Pope. Ever so lightly painted in the foreground is a mouse. A metaphor for the struggle that is the artistic life?

The Bull Moose Room celebrates Teddy Roosevelt and features framed Confederate bonds, an invitation to President Roosevelt's inauguration, and old drawings of New York during the 1800s, including one of the elevated trains that once ran through Herald Square.

Keens built its reputation as the city's premier spot for mutton. Because mutton has gone out of style, I'll define it: it's sheep meat. Not baby sheep— that's lamb—but full-grown, adult sheep meat. (Fun fact: intermediate sheep meat is called *hogget*.) From its opening in 1885 to about the 1940s, Keens served plate after plate of mutton. In fact, the restaurant celebrated its one-millionth order of mutton in 1935. Today, mutton, a supersized 26-ounce helping at Keens, is ordered by older diners who enjoyed the dish in years past or younger patrons who want to try something new. How many mutton-chops have been devoured at Keens since 1935? "It's safe to say at least another million," promises Jenkins.

Keens stores its meat in a dry-aging locker in the basement, where it becomes more flavorful and tender by the day. Just how much meat does Keens have on the premises? "A lot," Jenkins laughs. The summer day I visited Keens, the meat inventory weighed in at 27,000 pounds. And that number tends to climb in the busier fall and winter seasons. Keens begins cooking its meats at a very high temperature and then lowers the heat dramatically, a process that allows the meat to most effectively hold its juices. "We take great pride in being some of the first people who go to the meat purveyors," says Conley. All the meat is hand-selected.

A food reporter from *The New York Times* wrote about Keens in 1939, "They frown on trying to do anything the least bit fancy with a steak as to sauce or seasoning. They think a steak is too good a thing in itself to be tampered with." Indeed, sometimes less is more, an attitude that is "absolutely" still employed today according to Conley.

Despite its reputation for mutton, "Amazingly, filet mignon is the top seller," reports Jenkins. Classic side dishes like spinach, carrots, and potatoes grace the menu, along with a raw bar featuring oysters, clams, lobster, and shrimp. The restaurant serves an average of 575 meals a day and has been known to cook up 700 meals at its busiest.

Keens fell on hard times in the 1970s and closed in 1977. But a year later, it was back and better than ever under the direction of George Schwartz and his pop artist wife Kiki Kogelnik. They invested $1.4 million in the property, fully renovating and redecorating the joint. They mounted the thousands of pipes Keens had in storage on the ceiling and put art on every wall, including a naked portrait of an unknown subject by an unknown artist over the scotch bar downstairs. Known as Miss Keens, "She speaks to our history as a men's club," Conley acknowledges.

Today, men and women can relish the history of this smoke-free smoking club over mutton or other meat.

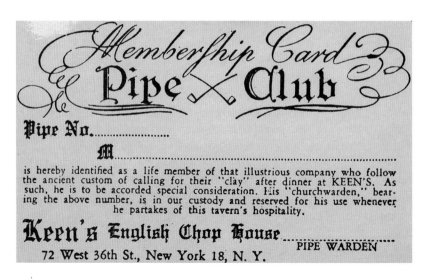

LOMBARDI'S PIZZA

32 SPRING ST, NEW YORK, NY 10012

(212) 941-7994 | WWW.FIRSTPIZZA.COM

It's hard to imagine a world without pizza. Without the promise of a pizza party, would your fourth grade class have ever behaved? Without a pizza pie, what would your family have eaten all those Friday nights? Luckily, if you're reading this, you were probably born after 1905, when customers could purchase the first pizzas in America at Little Italy staple Lombardi's.

·LOMBARDI'S in 1905·

The nation's first commercial pizza agent continues to dazzle customers with its delicious pies.

Ancient Romans, Greeks, and Egyptians concocted flatbread dishes, but the winning combination of dough, tomato sauce, and cheese was popular in Naples, a Greek settlement. Pizza flourished in Naples, Italy, during the 1800s. During a visit to Naples in 1889, King Umberto I and Queen Margherita enjoyed pizza pies. One story indicates that the Queen was so taken with the mozzarella, tomato, and basil pizza that this pie became known as the Margherita Pizza, a term still used today.

In the late nineteenth century, the war for Italian unification sent many displaced northern refugees to the United States, some of whom were skilled artisans looking for work. At the turn of the century, high rates of poverty, malnourishment, and disease drove unskilled Southern Italians to leave. Between 1880 and 1924, four million Italians immigrated to the United States. Half of these immigrants came in the first decade of the 20th century. Many Italians settled in New York City, creating a vibrant community called Little Italy. (For more on the discrimination that Italian Americans faced, see the entry about Ferdinando's Focacceria on page 141.)

One of these Italian immigrants was Gennaro Lombardi, who opened a grocery store on Spring Street in 1897. He sold tomato and cheese pizzas in his store for takeout. These pies became so popular that he decided to do away with the groceries and sell pizza exclusively. In 1905, he applied for a restaurant license and started the first commercial pizzeria in the United States.

Lombardi specialized in thin crust pizza baked in a coal-fired oven. This type of oven created a smoky crust that still defines Lombardi's pies. Although Lombardi originally sold individual slices, customers must order an entire pie today. The centerpiece of Lombardi's menu is its Margherita pizza. Like a world map, its red sauce looks like the ocean and its cheese provides partial coverage like continents. The pepperoni pizza features tiny buttons of pepperoni that curve slightly upward like Frisbees. And the white pizza is deliciously creamy.

In its early years, Italian workers on their lunch breaks formed the bulk of Lombardi's clientele. For a nickel, workers could enjoy a slice wrapped in paper. It was a fast, cheap, and easy lunch-break choice, with no utensils required. As pizza became increasingly popular in the United States, its customer base diversified. This happened mostly after World War II, when American soldiers who'd been stationed in Italy returned home hankering for a taste of this ethnic food they'd come to love.

More pizza-lovers also meant more competition. American GI Ira Nevin fell in love with pizza while stationed in Naples. His family was in the oven business, and upon his return, he invented the gas-fired ceramic pizza oven. These ovens proved a game-changer. Cleaner and more efficient than coal ovens, they made opening pizzerias an attractive option for Italian and non-Italian entrepreneurs alike.

Italians opened pizzerias when they moved to other cities for factory jobs. In metropolises like New Haven, Boston, and Trenton, pizzerias provided cheap food for hard-working families. There is perhaps no other food that is so easy to share as a pizza, and so it has remained a staple in social gatherings. Pizzas also became popular bar food. What better food to chase a shot with than a hearty slice of 'za?

More pizzerias meant more pizza fans. And pizza delivery and frozen pizzas transformed a once-ethnic food into an all-American meal. The pizza surpassed the hamburger as America's fast casual choice. The pizza parlor became the new candy store: the choice hangout for tweens and teens before they graduated to bars.

Like the bagel, pizza defines New York City's food culture. There are about 360 pizzerias in Manhattan. When Donald Trump showed Sarah Palin around New York City in 2011 what did they eat? Pizza. But their venture for a New York slice ended in an epic failure. They chose a generic chain (Famous Famiglia Pizzeria), and the Donald was caught eating his slice with a knife and fork. Real New Yorkers eat a slice with their hands.

Many of Lombardi's employees have branched out and opened their own pizzerias. John's Pizzeria on Bleecker Street, Patsy's Pizzeria in Harlem, and Totonno's Pizzerria Napolitano in Coney Island all grew in the hands of Lombardi's graduates.

Lombardi's closed in 1984 but reopened a decade later one block away on the same street.

Today, the clientele is a far cry from factory workers. "Now it's mostly visitors to New York City and some locals that live nearby," says General Manager Mike Giammarino.

Although Lombardi's has thrived for over a century, Little Italy has not. Not only has Little Italy gotten smaller and smaller over the years, but the percentage of Italians actually living in Little Italy has also dwindled. In the 1930s, Italians comprised 98 percent of Little Italy households. By 1950, that percentage declined to about 50 percent as Italians moved out to the suburbs. By 2000, the percentage of Italians in Little Italy dwindled to 6 percent. A decade later, the U.S. census revealed that just 5 percent of those living in Little Italy identified as Italian-American, and *none* of these residents had been born in Italy.

Chinatown has taken over more and more of the neighborhood, so much so that the neighborhoods are now grouped together as the Chinatown and Little Italy Historic District. Little Italy has "become a close sister to Chinatown," says Giammarino. An East Meets West Christmas Parade every year features both Italian and Chinese floats. Lombardi's, however, has survived the de-Italianization of Little Italy, one pizza pie at a time. So for a real slice of Italian cuisine, head to Lombardi's.

MCSORLEY'S OLD ALE HOUSE

15 EAST 7TH ST, NEW YORK, NY 10003

(212) 473-9148

This is the coolest bar I've ever been to," a Canadian visitor murmurs to his friend. To give his chum an authentic taste of New York, the local vetoed Times Square in favor of McSorley's Old Ale House. At McSorley's, sawdust covers the floors, and the walls display artifacts from Houdini's handcuffs to seasoned New York Fire Department helmets. In business since the mid-1800s, McSorley's is one of New York's oldest and best loved bars.

John McSorley opened this alehouse in 1862 and called it The Old House at Home. When the tavern sign blew down in 1908, McSorley took the opportunity to rename the bar after himself. (The sign today claims "Est. 1854," but there has been debate about McSorley's actual birthday, so we'll go with historian Richard McDermott's verdict that McSorley's dates back to 1862.) The tavern catered mostly to neighborhood workingmen and kept things utterly simple. No hard alcohol. And just two options: dark ale and light ale.

According to *The New Yorker*'s 1940 profile of McSorley's, "Old John" believed that a "man never lived who needed a stronger drink than a mug of stock ale warmed on the hob of a stove." Patrons who purchased ale received a free smoke from McSorley's collection of communal pipes and a complimentary lunch of crackers, onions, and cheese. John loved onions. He ate them like apples. Under his reign, a "no ladies" policy ruled. He believed that for men to drink in peace, they had to do so in the company of other men.

Old John passed the bar down to his son Old Bill, who earned his nickname because like his father, he was a crank. Old Bill detested noise and banged on a gong if the bar became too rowdy. On occasion, he also kept customers waiting while he read the newspaper. But his sourpuss routine actually won customers over. (Nice guys really can't win.)

Under Old Bill, McSorley's ignored Prohibition. The tavern brewed its own beer in the basement during those years, calling it "near beer," a literary loophole that satisfied customers and, apparently, the fuzz. The police never raided McSorley's during Prohibition, even though it was common knowledge that *near* beer was very much *on the nose* beer.

Bill wouldn't let women drink here, but he had no problem with felines. His cats had free reign of the tavern. Between 1912 and 1930 painter John Sloan created five paintings inspired by McSorley's, including one titled, *McSorley's Cats*. Legend has it that if you see a cat napping in the window, Houdini's spirit is roving the bar. Cats roamed the bar until a woman filed a lawsuit in 2010 alleging that a McSorley's cat attacked her. The Department of Health then cracked down on the cats.

After Old Bill, Daniel O'Connell became the owner. The retired police officer took the reins in 1936 and passed the bar down to his daughter, Dorothy O'Connell Kirwan, in 1940. Some feared that a female owner would bring unwanted change to the beloved neighborhood hangout, but Dorothy vowed to maintain the status quo, including the "no women" rule. She never even visited the bar during operating hours. For a century, the bar's slogan had been: "Good ale, raw onions, and no ladies." But that changed when lawyer Faith Seidenberg got on the case in 1969.

Only two women had technically been served at McSorley's before 1969. The first was a peanut vendor nicknamed Mother Fresh-Roasted who sold her goods at city saloons. Old John let her enjoy a mug of ale while she sold peanuts inside the bar. The second female was a woman who disguised herself as a man and was served ale in 1924 by Old Bill. After she drank her ale, the woman let down her hair, shocking Bill and sending him into a rage.

In 1969, Seidenberg and her friend Karen DeCrow entered McSorley's and asked to be served. Employees promptly escorted them to the door. But Seidenberg didn't take no for an answer. She sued. The following year, a judge ruled that public places could not discriminate based on sex, and McSorley's opened its doors to women.

Barbara Shaum became the first woman to drink at McSorley's under this new law in 1970. Shaum operated a leather shop two doors down from McSorley's and had many friends at the tavern. McSorley's then-manager, Daniel O'Connell-Kirwan, invited Shaum to be their first official female customer. She donned a straw hat, took his arm, and waltzed into the tavern. Beer equality for all had been won.

A new slogan was in order. The institution settled on: "We were here before you were born." For patrons who've been drinking for seven decades and those just earning the legal right to imbibe, the slogan fits.

O'Connell-Kirwan took over McSorley's in 1975 before selling to current owner Matthew Maher in 1977. In 1994, Maher's daughter Theresa Delahaba became the bar's first female bartender. Two decades later, she's still slinging ale. "I'm here twenty-one years and people say 'Oh my God, I can't believe they put a girl behind the bar,'" she recounts. But while the environment is certainly male-dominated, she's been fitting right in since her childhood when she accompanied her father to work or washed dishes in the kitchen.

Although she's technically the manager, Delahaba shies away from the title, arguing that with staff that has been here for ten to thirty years, "the place runs itself. It's not rocket science."

Indeed, McSorley's simple menu makes the joint easy to run. Even with the large groups that often choose McSorley's for get-togethers, it's easy to serve a big group when they're only getting ale.

A brief lesson on ale: It's is a type of beer. So is lager. The main difference between ale and lager is the fermentation process, which yields differences in taste and smell. Ale uses *Saccharomyces cerevisiae* yeast, and lager uses *Saccharomyces pastorianus* yeast. Ale's yeast ferments quickly on the *top* in a warm climate, and lager's yeast ferments on the *bottom* in a cold climate over a longer period of time. The difference results in ale's fruitier taste.

Be sure to look up at the chandelier draped with wishbones over the bar. Soldiers going to fight in World War I hung these wishbones on the chandelier for good luck. If a man made it back alive he took his wishbone down. The wishbones still hanging mean that a solider never made it home. For years and years, the wishbones collected dust. So much dust had gathered that health inspectors gave McSorley's a hard time. Matthew Maher finally washed them one day, much to the protest of some customers who weren't too keen on change. "Quite a few customers gave their opinion on that . . . " Delahaba trails off.

Everywhere you look, there's something new to see. Joe Kennedy's boots hanging from the ceiling. A wanted poster for John Wilkes Booth. A

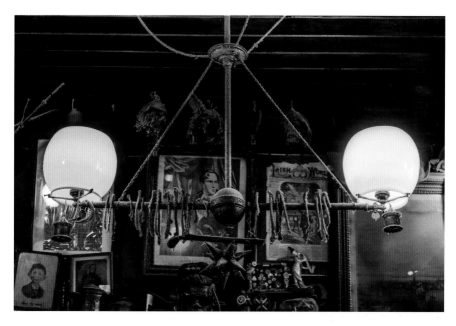

tribute to firefighters lost on 9/11. Memories cover every inch of wall space. The bar can get insanely crowded on a weekend night, so if you want to take a good look at all the walls have to offer, opt for a daytime visit.

McSorley's managed to stay in business in the same location for all these years in part because every owner has bought the building. And the bar's dedication to consistency, from its menu—the kitchen is known for its cheese plate, burgers, and chili—to its appearance, also makes it a destination to visit again.

"I never want this place to change," says Delahaba. With her nephews coming of age and expressing interest in the business, the bar is likely to stay in her family. And with crowds young to old filling the rustic space, it's on track to keep providing New Yorkers an authentic hotspot to take out-of-town visitors or enjoy an ale-filled night out.

NOM WAH TEA PARLOR

13 DOYERS STREET, NEW YORK, NY 10013

(212) 962-6047 | NOMWAH.COM

It was the bloodiest intersection in America: The boomerang-shaped street in Chinatown served as a battlefield for rival Chinese gangs at the beginning of the twentieth century. Known as the "Bloody Angle," the street's bend afforded an element of surprise as well as escape routes via tunnels connected to the street's buildings. The days of this street's violence are long gone, so it's known now simply by its official name: Doyers Street. It remains an important street not for gang violence, but for food. For here, in the middle of this bent road, operates the Nom Wah Tea Parlor, a circa 1920 dim sum producer extraordinaire.

China and the United States have had a long and changing relationship. China explored the seas in the fifteenth century but then went into a period of isolation and had little interest in the Western world. In 1793, Qing dynasty Emperor Quian Long wrote to King George III, "China possesses all things . . . and has no use for your country's manufactures." But China didn't have opium. So Great Britain illegally exported it from India to China, leading to widespread addiction that wreaked havoc on China's social and economic climate. Tension between the two empires led to the First Opium War (1839–1842). The treaty that ended the war gave Hong Kong to Great Britain and increased the number of ports where Great Britain could trade from one to five.

The Second Opium War (1856–1860) pitted Great Britain and France against China. Around this time, Chinese immigration to the United States began in earnest. Jobs building the transcontinental railroad and the Gold Rush lured Chinese immigrants to the United States' West Coast in the mid-1800s. A sign in Southern China advertised opportunities in the United States: *"Americans are very rich people. They want the Chinaman to come*

and make him very welcome. There you will have great pay, large houses, and food and clothing of the finest description . . . . It is a nice country, without Mandarins or soldiers. All alike; big man no larger than little man."

By 1880, about 350 Chinese immigrants had settled in lower Manhattan, laying the foundation for the city's Chinatown. They created the Chinese Consolidated Benevolent Association, essentially their own government. Self-segregation provided a defense against rampant discrimination.

In a tale as old as time, Americans feared that Chinese immigrants would take their jobs, leading to great anti-Chinese sentiment. In 1882, Congress passed the Chinese Exclusion Act, which barred Chinese immigrants already in the country from becoming citizens and impeded the immigration of all Chinese citizens except merchants, students, and diplomats. This meant that Chinese workers in the United States could not bring their family members over to join them. This created extreme gender imbalance, or a "bachelor society." In 1900, only 40 to 150 Chinese women lived in Manhattan, compared to the 7,000 Chinese men that lived here. Some Chinese men turned to prostitutes in the wake of a less than ideal dating climate, leading to further anti-Chinese sentiment.

Americans used the generic names "John" and "Charlie Chinaman" for all Chinese immigrants. "John" typically referred to a merchant, while

"Charlie Chinaman" referred to lower classes. Yellow face performances, the ugly cousin of blackface, dehumanized Chinese people in racist shows. Americans searched for ways to make Chinese labor obsolete or get rid of Chinese residents altogether. For instance, Edward A. Smith invented the Iron Chink in 1903. (*Chink* is a derogatory term used for Chinese people). The machine could gut and clean salmon for canning fifty-five times faster than a man. Many Chinese men found employment in the canning industry, so the invention promised to eliminate the need for their labor. Communities held meetings to try to solve the "Chinese question."

Faced with racist employers who would not hire them, many Chinese immigrants opened their own laundries and restaurants. Restaurants played an important role in introducing Americans to Chinese culture. The trick for success was often creating dishes and environments that were both intriguing in their difference but comfortable in their familiarity. In the late 1800s, this meant chop suey. This dish brought many New Yorkers downtown to Chinatown.

By 1920, gang violence no longer plagued Doyers Street, and it was a good location to open a business. And that's what the owners of the Nom Wah Tea Parlor did. The establishment began as a bakery but has morphed into the city's go-to destination for dim sum.

Literally translated, dim sum means "to touch your heart." It is a term that generally describes the small steamed or deep-fried dishes, most notably steamed dumplings, for which the place has gained recognition. Similar to tapas, dim sum traditionally consists of small plates of food, usually paired with tea. Dim sum's roots can be traced to Canton, a southern province of China, where travelers on the Silk Road stopped at roadside establishments offering steamed dumplings and tea.

Nom Wah built on this history. The original owners are unknown, but Ed and May Choy operated the business in the 1940s. For the next forty years, Nom Wah's bakery dominated business, particularly its famous moon cake, a lotus paste and red bean-filled pastry. This pastry was a top seller

during the annual Chinese Mid-Autumn Festival, a harvest celebration of the moon's impact on agriculture involving sacrifices to the moon that dates back to about 250 B.C. But as more bakeries opened in Chinatown, Nom Wah shifted its focus to other dishes. Today, the restaurant is best known for its dumplings.

The United States terminated the Chinese Exclusion Act in 1943. By then, World War II had exploded and the United States had an ally in China, both having been attacked by Japan. Thirteen thousand Chinese Americans served in the U.S. Army. During World War II, American attitudes toward the Chinese improved, especially as the "good Chinese" were contrasted with the "bad Japanese." Chinese immigrant and journalist Charlie Leong wrote, "To the men of our generation, World War II was the most important historical event of our times. For the first time, we felt we could make it in American society." The repeal of the Chinese Exclusion Act in 1943 saw great increases in Chinese immigration from Mainland China, Taiwan, and Hong Kong.

Ed and May Choy's nephew, Wally Tang, immigrated to New York in 1950 at age 16 and started working in Nom Wah's kitchen. In 1976, he bought the restaurant from his aunt and uncle. Today, Wally's nephew Wilson Tang owns and runs the business. He even opened a second Nom Wah in Philadelphia in 2015.

New York City's Nom Wah wears its age. The yellow walls are faded. The geometric tiles on the floor bear the marks of many soles. The decor is decidedly unpolished and disjointed. Two paper lanterns hang over the cash register. Two mismatched paintings hang near the world's tiniest restrooms. Red booths hug two walls and tables clutter the center of the restaurant. The humble atmosphere befits its ties to Chinese immigrants who came to this country at the turn of the century for a piece of the American dream.

Nom Wah's tea selection is vast and interesting. The Bo-lay tea is the top seller. Other teas include bitter tea known for helping digestion, weight loss, and sore throats; and there's oolong tea, which reportedly promotes a youthful appearance.

The dessert menu has been narrowed to just two offerings: a crunchy almond cookie and a fried sesame ball filled with lotus paste. Not overly sweet, the sesame balls provide a great mixture of textures by combining paste, dough, and seeds.

The menu highlights dim sum but also offers entrees like scallion pancakes and rice rolls. The vegetarian rice rolls pair a squishy, filmy exterior with celery, carrot, and mushroom filling to create a mild dish. The scallion pancakes are excellent. Presented like triangle quesadillas, the pancakes are crunchy, pan-fried, and drizzled with sauce. Other options include spring rolls, spare ribs, fried rice, and turnip cake. For a quick introduction to dim sum, try the steamed or fried dim sum samplers, aesthetically beautiful arrangements that are served in small round tins.

With its close streets and specialty wares, Chinatown offers a unique city within a city. And Nom Wah offers a tasty slice of Chinese American history.

OLD HOMESTEAD STEAKHOUSE

56 NINTH AVE, NEW YORK, NY 10011

(212) 242-9040 | WWW.THEOLDHOMESTEADSTEAKHOUSE.COM

The Old Homestead Steakhouse puts the meat in the meatpacking district. The iconic steakhouse on Ninth Avenue has been satisfying carnivores since 1868. Look for the cow perched above its entrance and enter a meat mecca.

The meatpacking district is known for its trendy restaurants and high fashion boutiques, but a century ago, 250 slaughterhouses and meat packing plants operated in this neighborhood. The sight of men in bloodstained white coats, meat trucks, and hanging carcasses defined the neighborhood. It's even rumored that because so much livestock came into this neighborhood, the city built a "cow tunnel" underground to shuttle cattle. But the neighborhood has undergone "a complete evolution," says Old Homestead co-owner Greg Sherry. "The days of the meatpacking are over." In the 1970s, gay leather bars, sex clubs, and dance halls populated the area, and you could find drugs or a prostitute on the corner. In the 1990s, high-end restaurants and retailers began to infiltrate the area. The meatpackers took a back seat to women in stilettos ungracefully maneuvering the cobblestoned streets.

Today, just five meatpacking companies operate in this district. Former City Council Member Christine Quinn told The Meatpacking District Improvement Association, "If you had said twenty years ago that the Meatpacking District is going to be a cultural hub, people would have looked at you like you were in some kind of beef-induced overdose haze and you had lost your mind." But that's exactly what it's become. Great restaurants, retail, the Whitney Museum, and the High Line have converged to make the Meat Packing District a cultural destination.

Amidst all this change, the Old Homestead has remained a relative constant. "The world has changed, but our steaks haven't," explains co-owner Marc Sherry, Greg's younger brother.

The restaurant grew from five tables and a bar to three floors that can accommodate 225 people and can serve between 500 and 800 customers on a typical night. About seven decades ago, dishwasher Harry Sherry climbed the ranks to become the restaurant's owner. His grandsons Greg and Marc learned the business under his tutelage and took the reins in 1972. The Brooklyn-born brothers remain in charge today as partners.

Jazz plays overhead while patrons dine in the dimly lit rooms at red booths and tables. The first floor features a bar and seating area where parallel rows of wide oval mirrors hang on stately dark wooden walls. Simple rectangular prism-and-cylinder light fixtures illuminate the room. The second floor features a small private room for celebrations and a library seating area where old books, photos, and trophies create a romantic setting. A third floor opens when demand necessitates. The decor is simple and refined. Perhaps this is so that your senses can focus on the true star: the meat.

"We are strictly prime in every cut that we have," promises Marc. If you're not sure exactly what that means, the United States Department of Agriculture can clear it up: Prime beef is "produced from young, well-fed beef cattle" and has "abundant marbling (the amount of fat interspersed with lean meat)." Meat with no marbling would appear all red, while meat with "abundant marbling" contains lots of white marks that resemble veins or a highway map. The restaurant has about 10,000 pounds of prime meat on the premises in any week.

The menu features filet mignon, rib steak, a T-bone steak, and more. I have eaten at a lot of steakhouses. There are even other steakhouses in this book. But none hold a candle to the filet mignon *au poivre* I devoured at the Old Homestead. My knife cut the tender meat so easily, and the peppercorn crust provided a perfect, complementary texture. The orange and red sauce creates a beautiful color palate. Portions are large, so large in fact, that Old

Homestead claims to have invented the doggy bag for leftovers. The menu also includes classic steakhouse sides like creamed and sautéed spinach, mashed potatoes, bacon, and buttermilk onion rings.

For $350, you can try twelve ounces of legendary Kobe beef. The Sherry brothers played an instrumental role in bringing Kobe beef from Japan to the United States: Kobe beef hails from—you guessed it—Kobe, Japan. Technically, it's called *Wagyu* beef. The cattle in Kobe eat a strict diet of grain, rice, soybeans, and beer. They receive a massage every day to disperse their fat evenly. Their handlers keep them from grazing. The lack of exercise keeps their muscle content low and their fat content high. Their daily habits result in 30 to 40 percent more marbling than USDA prime beef.

After tasting Kobe beef in Japan, Greg and Marc knew they wanted to bring it to the United States. But to do so, they had to get Japanese producers to meet USDA requirements. They worked with these producers to upgrade their facilities and meet USDA sanitation codes. By 1991, the Old Homestead became the first restaurant in the United States to serve Kobe beef. The accomplishment earned Greg and Marc the nickname the "Ambassadors of Steak." Back then, the Old Homestead served a 16-ounce Kobe beefsteak for $100. Today, the portion has been downsized to twelve ounces and its price hiked to $350. The beef was banned in the United States from 2001 to 2006 and from 2010 to 2012. But today, for about $20 a bite, you can taste the pampered, fatty beef, or indulge in a Kobe beef burger for $81.

Through Greg and Marc's efforts, the Old Homestead Steakhouse has achieved brand recognition in Japan. So it's only fitting that the Sherry brothers will open an Old Homestead in Tokyo. This international expansion will follow two domestic expansions to Atlantic City and Las Vegas. But expansion is a very recent development. "We were a single unit [and] happy with it," reflects Marc. That changed when the owner of the Borgata Hotel Casino and Spa in Atlantic City approached the brothers about opening a restaurant in the resort. Greg and Marc liked that they were "close enough that we could watch" and forged ahead with the project. "Once every 135 years we like to shake it up a little bit," Marc jokes. Three years ago, the co-owners expanded once more to Caesars Palace in Las Vegas. Arguably harder to reach from New York than Atlantic City, Greg and Marc approach their expansions and daily operations with a hands-on attitude.

Each branch displays a distinct piece of art. Here in New York, that's the cow mounted outside. Her name is Annabelle. She's been with the restaurant since Greg and Marc's grandfather ran the place. A farmer from Nebraska sent Harry the cow. He decided to put it above the restaurant's entrance. And there she's stayed for over six decades, with "a couple of nips and tucks along the way," according to Marc. The Las Vegas restaurant displays Annabelle's sister, and the Atlantic City restaurant features a commissioned painting of Annabelle by famous artist Julian Schnabel.

The restaurant's clientele has become more balanced in the last decade. Ten years ago, Greg estimates New York's lunch business, for instance, broke down to 90 percent male and 10 percent female. Today, he estimates that it has evolved to about 60 percent male and 40 percent female. No matter who's in the restaurant, Marc believes they're the kind of people you want to rub shoulders with. "If you sat at the bar for one year, you'd meet everyone you'd want to meet," he argues. On a November afternoon, I dined next to a pair of television producers and a trio of men negotiating a roundabout business deal.

In 2010, the Old Homestead merged the neighborhood's interests in meat and fashion by designing a meat dress of their own after Lady Gaga infamously wore a dress made of meat to the 2010 MTV Video Music Awards. Greg and Marc took issue with the pop star's dress because it was made from flank steaks rather than the prime beef they favored. So the brothers commissioned a higher quality meat dress made from prime porterhouse steak and pork rib eye. The end result weighed 85 pounds and went on the market for $100,000. No one has ponied up the cash yet, so it's being stored in a freezer at a secret location.

Interested parties can feel free to inquire. Meat lovers would be wise to head to the Old Homestead Steakhouse. Meat dress-optional.

OLD TOWN BAR

45 E 18TH ST, NEW YORK, NY 10003

(212) 529-6732 | WWW.OLDTOWNBAR.COM

It's in the name. Old Town Bar is really old. It's been pouring beers since 1892, and not much has changed since then. Tiled hexagons and squares create a floor that thousands have pounded in search of booze and conversation. The bar's high tin ceilings, booths, and long mahogany bar wear their age with grace and appeal. Chandeliers are no longer lit by gas, but they still shine with seasoned charm. This no-frills New York institution has survived an ever-changing city by sticking to the basics: beer, burgers, and people.

The bar opened under the name Viermeisters and served German fare during the first half of the twentieth century. The Lohden family ran the bar for a few decades, followed by the current family, the Meaghers. Larry Meagher started out as a manager of Old Town in the late 1960s and then became the owner. Today, his son Gerard Meagher co-owns the joint with his siblings and acts as the general manager.

Meagher says that one of Old Town's strengths is its ability to attract a diverse clientele. "New York has become very segmented," he observes. "[There are] places that appeal to gay guys or places that appeal to hipsters [or] places that appeal to Wall Street guys. We have a place that anybody can walk in and feel comfortable." Meagher credits the bar's low-key, quirky atmosphere and its reasonable prices as draws for its all-inclusive brand of patrons. "[There's] no typical Old Town customer," he says.

The unpredictable clientele makes running Old Town a joy to Meagher. "It's not just the same twenty guys every day," he says. The bar does have its regulars and its "irregular regulars" as Meagher puts it. He doesn't like to play favorites, but he does have a soft spot for writers. "The writers come here because it's a place you can talk," he reveals. Old Town has no televisions or loud music, so you can not only talk, but think as well. Meagher also fought for a no cell phones policy, but "we had to declare ourselves the loser" in that fight he says. Still, writers like Frank McCourt (*Angela's Ashes, 'Tis*) and poet Seamus Heaney wrote in Old Town. McCourt even signed a poster on the second floor, "To The Old Town—The King of New York Bars—Where You Can Still Talk!"

Old Town built its food reputation around the hamburger. The restaurant has used the same meat vendor for the last thirty-four years, and homemade fries accompany the generously sized patties. Meagher recalls when members of the New York Jets came in to Old Town after a game. "One hamburger plate was enough for them." Chances are if that's true, one plate will be more than satisfying for you.

Old Town Bar operated as a speakeasy by the name of Craig's Restaurant during Prohibition. The booths provided hiding spots for booze under the seats. The headquarters of the Tammany Hall political machine were nearby from 1929 to 1943, and according to Meagher, there's no record that they were ever busted for booze. Does that mean Democratic cronies were breaking the law here? "Chances are they did," he guesses.

Old Town still uses a dumb-waiter to lower food from the second-floor kitchen down to the first floor, a journey of approximately fifteen seconds. The second floor dining area contains booths and tables as well as an eclectic array of artwork, including a series of paintings that feature monks making wine, a random portrait of George Washington, and memorabilia from TV and film productions that have filmed at Old Town, including *Mad About You* and *The Devil's Own*. Women were once limited to the second floor, so that's where the women's restroom remains. It's nothing to write home about, unlike the men's room downstairs. . . .

Old Town Bar's urinals are famous. So celebrated are these urinals that Old Town hosted a one hundredth birthday celebration for the men's room gems in 2010. What's so special about these Hinsdale urinals? Let's go back to the very beginning. Going to the bathroom was once a solitary

act. Outhouses provided a room for one to conduct one's "business." But as immigration surged and indoor plumbing became all the rage, relieving oneself inside came into vogue. The first patented urinal dates back to 1866. But space is money, so trench and trough-style urinals emerged as products of efficiency and technology. An act that had once been private was thrust into the public sphere.

Winfield E. Hinsdale patented his own Hinsdale Urinals on November 1, 1901. While some urinals offer little sense of privacy, Hinsdale urinals essentially wrap around the user, creating a sense of solitude in a communal setting. They're large, creating an ample buffer for even the largest of gentlemen.

"The bathrooms in New York tend to be squeezed into corners," says Meagher. Indeed, New York real estate is so expensive that most businesses want to optimize every square foot. But Old Town's men's room dates back to 1910, when New York was far less crowded. Meagher says Old Town's urinals offer "comfort, privacy, and beauty."

Mayor Michael Bloomberg agreed. When Old Town threw a birthday party for its urinals, Bloomberg sent the following letter, which hangs in a frame at Old Town today:

Dear Gerard:

It has come to my attention that you are holding a 100th birth-day celebration for one of our city's unofficial landmarks, and one of the Old Town Bar's most essential, most admired, most gazed upon, and most trickled upon fixtures: the legendary Hinsdales.

These regal receptacles have, for an entire century, through war and peace, triumphs and tribulations, witnessed man in all his glory. They have seen a steady stream of actors and artists, poets and politicians, sailors and sandhogs—and welcomed all with open drains. Countless customers have left their seats to see a man about a horse—and the Hinsdales have allowed them to do so in great style.

Even after 100 years of use, with customers constantly taking direct aim at them, these porcelain palaces are still standing tall, still working day and night. And I speak for all New Yorkers when I say: What a relief!

Thank you for preserving a piece—emphasis on the letter p—of our history. And may the Hinsdales be comforting customers at the Old Town Bar for another 100 years to come.

Sincerely,

Michael R. Bloomberg, Mayor

Bloomberg wasn't the only prominent figure to praise Old Town's urinals. *Sports Illustrated* writer Steve Rushin was on hand to give a toilet toast. Rushin had previously praised Old Town's urinals in a column in which he detailed the nostalgia for ballpark trough urinals and the challenges of one-size-fits-all urinals for children at sporting events. He argued that the journey from stall to urinal was as monumental for a young boy as going to your first ballgame. Rushin described Old Town's urinals as "the greatest achievements in porcelain since Belleek made its first tea set."

So if you want a beer, a burger, or you just really have to "go," consider Old Town Bar. No matter what crowd you roll with, you'll fit right in.

ONE IF BY LAND, TWO IF BY SEA

17 BARROW STREET, NEW YORK, NY 10014

(212) 255-8649 | ONEIFBYLAND.COM

I t's been one of New York City's most romantic restaurants since 1973. But before that, it was a silent movie house. And before *that*, it was Aaron Burr's carraige house.

The inconspicuous entrance to One If By Land, Two If By Sea makes this candlelit escape somewhat hidden. The brick building features twin wooden doors on either side of twin windows surrounded by wood paneling. Sadly, a beautiful white archway above the entrance has been removed.

The restaurant's logo of a man straddling a horse raised up on its hind legs decorates each door. As the restaurant's name suggests, this rider is Paul Revere, the man who warned his community how the British were coming: one lantern to indicate the Redcoats approached on foot and two lanterns if they approached by boat.

The entrance leads directly into a bar and sitting area where a pianist works the keys. Beyond this small lounge is the main dining room. Its extremely high ceiling creates ample space for the restaurant's many chandeliers. White tablecloths, tall stand-alone candles, and bouquets of flowers adorn each table. Upstairs, a small dining area features replicas of Hamilton's and Burr's dueling pistols behind a display case.

Aaron Burr never quite achieved his dreams. He has a long list of accolades—Attorney General of the United States, U.S. Senator, U.S. Vice President—but his chief goal of becoming President of the United States always eluded him. In his poem *Harlem*, Langston Hughes asks, "What happens to a dream deferred?" The final rhyme hypothesizes, "Maybe it just sags like a heavy load. Or does it explode?" In the case of Aaron Burr's deferred dreams, they simply exploded.

Burr and Hamilton had a contentious history as political rivals and personal nemeses. Burr belonged to the Republican Party, and Hamilton belonged to the Federalist party. When Burr ran for president in 1800, Hamilton worked to get Burr's opponent, Thomas Jefferson, elected. Jefferson won the election, and Burr became vice president instead. (Back then, the runner-up became VP.) Burr certainly didn't appreciate Hamilton's efforts to block his ascension to the Oval Office. Hamilton also had a history of insulting Burr in the press. At one point, Hamilton stated that Burr's "public principles have no other spring or aim than his own aggrandizement," and called him "embryo-Caesar." He also said Burr was "unprincipled both as a public and private man."

Those were fighting words in 1804. Or, rather, dueling words. Burr demanded that Hamilton apologize for insulting his character. When

Hamilton did not, Burr challenged him to a duel. New York had made dueling illegal, so the men met a short trip away in Weehawken, New Jersey. Hamilton's son had actually died in a duel two years earlier in the same spot. His son's death motivated Hamilton to pass the law making dueling illegal in New York. It's interesting to note that Burr had faced Hamilton's brother-in-law in a duel in 1799.

Dying in a duel was actually pretty unlikely. The rules of dueling encouraged participants to reach a peaceful resolution to a disagreement. The 1777 Code Duello outlined these rules, which include calls for apology, weapon choice, time of day, etc. The Code stated that duels should never be fought at night, "for it is desirable to avoid all hot-headed proceedings." But what appeared as a way to peacefully resolve disagreements, in fact, was a loophole in the law to get away with murder.

On July 11, 1804, Burr shot Hamilton. Hamilton died the following day in New York. Both New York and New Jersey charged Burr with murder. The sitting vice president was never found guilty, but public opinion did turn against him.

After the duel, Burr pursued a crazy scheme: He tried to take over territory west of the Mississippi and become its emperor. He teamed with Army Commander-in-Chief James Wilkinson to seize the Louisiana Territory. In 1806 Burr led an army toward New Orleans. But Wilkinson turned against Burr and reported their scheme to the government. Burr was charged with treason in 1807. He escaped conviction but fled to Europe to get away from angry American opinion, which had turned against him. But his quest for power did not die along with his reputation. From Europe he concocted another plan to seize American territory, but it never materialized. Burr eventually returned to New York to practice law. He died in 1836.

Dining at One If By Land certainly conjures thoughts of this controversial man's life. The restaurant's high prices match its romantic, upscale atmosphere. When ordering à la carte, a two-course minimum is required,

beginning with items like a Cippolini Onion Tart or foie gras before moving on to entrees like a Chilean Sea Bass and a rack of pork that will set you back around $50 to $60 dollars. The three-course prix-fixe menu is $95 a head. If you're up for eleven courses, try the Chef's tasting menu for $165 or a 6-course option for $95 or $120. Wine pairings drive the cost up an additional $60 or $90. A jazz brunch offers a more affordable afternoon for $39 a person (not including alcoholic beverages or dessert). The first course offers pastries and baked goods, the second course features salad, soup, granola, and oatmeal, while the third course features entrees like Banana Stuffed French Toast or a hamburger with foie gras and wild mushrooms.

The dark, candlelit atmosphere at One If By Land sets up an evening for romance, but whether or not you have a significant other in tow, the building's historic background warrants a trip.

PETE'S TAVERN

129 EAST 18TH STREET, NEW YORK, NY 10003-2401

(212) 473-7676 | WWW.PETESTAVERN.COM

I n an old house in Paris that was covered with vines lived twelve little girls in two straight lines." The words had been scribbled on the back of a menu left behind at Pete's Tavern, a popular watering hole that wrapped around the block at 18th Street and Irving Place. The line would go on to become the iconic opening rhyme to *Madeline*, the popular children's book and eventual series by Ludwig Bemelmans.

Bemelmans lived in the Hotel Irving near Pete's Tavern and ordered from the Italian menu here almost every night, often in the company of his wife, Madeleine, and daughter Barbara. Inspired by the women in his life and his own experiences as a small boy, Bemelmans wrote down these lines, and the characters, Madeleine and her caretaker Miss Clavel, came to life. Bemelmans left the menu behind but kept the rhyme in his head. It went on to open every single *Madeline* story that was ever published.

Well before *Madeline* burst onto the literary scene in 1939, Pete's Tavern served as the birthplace for another literary work, O. Henry's short story *Gift of the Magi*. This led to the inscription on one of Pete's black awnings: "The Tavern O. Henry Made Famous." "O. Henry" was actually a pseudonym employed by William Sydney Porter, who launched his writing career with a penname from prison. Porter spent his three-year sentence for embezzlement writing short stories. By the time he earned early release in 1901, he had built a solid reputation as O. Henry. He moved to New York City in 1902 and settled at 55 Irving Place across the street from Pete's. He became a regular, and in 1903, while sitting in the first booth, penned *Gift of the Magi*. The *New York World* published the story two years later. It focuses on a New York City couple trying to buy each other secret Christmas presents

without overspending. In trademark O. Henry style, it features ordinary people and a surprise ending. To honor Pete's contributions to the literary world, the New York Library awarded Pete's a "Friends of the Libraries" plaque in 1999.

So, what's the next great literary work to be written at Pete's? "We see a lot of people with laptops [at Pete's]," says General Manager Declan Gaffney, but so far, none have risen to prominence since O. Henry and Bemelmans. However, the bar's artistic vibe *has* lured production teams from *Seinfeld*, *Law and Order*, and *Sex and the City* to film here, along with films such as the original *Endless Love* and a couple of beer commercials.

The building dates back to 1829 when it housed the Portman Hotel. The tavern's second room was a horse stable at the time. In 1864, it became and would always be a drinking establishment. Tom and John Healy purchased the building in 1899 and named it Healy's Café. Twenty-three years later, Peter D'Belles assumed ownership and named it after himself: Pete's Tavern. The name hasn't changed since. Neither has much else.

The physical space, its trappings, and atmosphere have remained basically constant since 1864. The forty-foot rosewood bar, front booths, tin ceiling, and tile floor are all originals. So is a large brass chandelier that hangs above the cash register. A large outdoor cafe provides a sunnier option than the dim and dark interior that embodies a sense of Old New York. What's one thing that has changed? The upstairs party room once served as a holding pen for livestock in Ringling, Barnum, and Bailey Circus, but don't expect to find any clowns or animals up there now.

Pete's clientele has always run the gamut. "It's not specific to any one genre or event," says Gaffney. Pete's is a place to bring your grandparents, to woo a first date, to break up, to celebrate, or commiserate. From drinks to a full Italian meal, Pete's is great for a pop-in or lengthy sit-down.

Gaffney has been with Pete's since he came to New York from Ireland in 1987. As a teenager, he worked in a hotel as a dishwasher. "I was absolutely mesmerized by the noise and the screaming and the shouting in the

kitchen," he recalls. "From that moment on I never wanted to do anything else." He rose through the ranks at Pete's from busboy to general manager over the last quarter century, and posits, "The only thing that's different between Pete's Tavern in 1987 and Pete's Tavern in 2015 are the pictures of celebrities on the wall and flat-screen TVs."

The menu features classic Italian fare. Top sellers include the prime rib, salmon steak, chicken parmigiana, and penne a la vodka. I personally enjoyed the spaghetti arrabbiatta made with olives, peppers, capers, and tomato sauce expertly providing a spicy kick.

Pete's also features an expansive drink menu. "I don't think people come here for the cocktails," says Gaffney, "[but they are] pleasantly surprised." Plenty of martinis, single malt scotches, champagnes, and wines diversify the menu. Gaffney's wife is partial to the Pineapple Jerry, which combines Sailor Jerry Spiced rum with Licor 43, pineapple juice, sour mix, and cinnamon. If you want to stick to the basics, try Pete's very own ale. Brewed in upstate New York, Pete's 1864 Ale is refreshing and light amber in color.

During Prohibition, Pete's ale flowed almost as freely as it does today. Pete's transformed itself into a flower shop during Prohibition, selling roses, orchids, violets, and gardenias in its front room and alcohol in the back.

Take a close look at the doorframe through which you enter Pete's second railway-style room, and you'll see a set of hinges. This is where a fake refrigerator door once stood that separated Pete's fully functioning flower shop and its not-so-secret alcohol sales. Pete's remained largely untouched by the police during Prohibition because many politicians breaking the law did so here.

Tammany Hall, the Democratic Party's unofficial headquarters from 1929 to 1943, was right around the corner from Pete's at 100 East 17th Street. Best known for its support of universal voting rights and its efforts to help the poor and immigrants (especially the Irish), The Hall also became infamous for its corrupt politics. Business meetings and other dealings often went down at Pete's over drinks, and the police—perhaps in the pockets of those making these deals—knew to steer clear. "Nobody would pretty much touch the place," concurs Gaffney. Once Prohibition ended, Pete's bid farewell to the flora and resumed food and beverage service in its front room. (For more on Tammany Hall, see the entry on Tweed's Restaurant and Buffalo Bar on page 170.)

Pete's tag line claims, "Sooner or later, everyone comes to Pete's." So screenwriters, playwrights, and listicle-writers of New York: Ditch your corner coffee shop and head to Pete's. There's a plaque that proves that this is a place where good things happen to those who write.

P.J. CLARKE'S

915 THIRD AVENUE AT 55TH STREET, NEW YORK, NY 10022

(212) 317-1616 | PJCLARKES.COM

This is literally as old school New York as you can get," the man seated at the table beside me remarks to his lunch date. In a sea of skyscrapers and modern, sleek restaurants, P.J. Clarke's feels old and classic. Maybe that's because it is. Since 1884, New Yorkers have been coming here for their beer and booze. Over a century later, big band music plays overhead, and classic American dishes are served at tables with red-and-white-checkered tablecloths in a timeless atmosphere.

The building dates back to 1868. A restaurant named Hennings opened here in 1884 owned by Mr. Jennings, whose first name remains a mystery. In

1902, P.J. Clarke immigrated to New York from Ireland and became a bartender under the second owner of the restaurant, Mr. Duneen, whose first name is also unknown. Clarke tended bar until 1912, when he bought the restaurant and named it after himself.

The Lavezzos family, who operated an antique business above P.J. Clarke's, bought the restaurant in 1948. As skyscrapers began to pop up all over the neighborhood, P.J. Clarke's found itself in a David and Goliath situation when developers wanted to commandeer the property. But the Lavezzos secured a 99-year lease for P.J. Clarke's, saving the business—only to go bankrupt.

Restaurateur Philip Scotti paired with Arnold Penner and a team of investors that includes actor Timothy Hutton and Yankees owner George Steinbrenner to save P.J. Clarke's from extinction in 2002. They closed for a year to renovate, worrying the bar's change-resistant regulars. But the regulars needn't have worried as Scotti and his crew wanted to spruce the place up, not change it. As he told the *New York Post* in 2003, "No way did I want this to be a refinished bar. It took 100 years to get all that smoke stain and beer stain and liquor stain on there, and I wanted to keep it that way."

Over the years, P.J. Clarke's has attracted a steady stream of famous clients. Elizabeth Taylor and Jackie Kennedy Onassis ate here. Nat King Cole famously called P.J.'s burgers "the Cadillac of burgers," and Buddy Holly proposed to his wife here with a ring inserted around a rose stem. Frank Sinatra spent a considerable amount of time at table 20. Johnny Mercer scribbled his future hit song "One For My Baby (and One for the Road)" on a napkin at P.J. Clarke's. After his famous New Year's Eve broadcasts, Dick Clark usually kicked off the start of his new year with a burger at P.J.'s. Actor Richard Harris (the original Dumbledore, for young readers) routinely ordered six double vodkas here. And after meeting a woman at P.J.'s, Dave Matthews penned his song "Stolen Away on 55th & 3rd," the restaurant's address. The celebrity draw seems steady. Seth Rogen sat a few tables away from me on an October afternoon. But celebrities are not a reason

to come here. For the big guy and the little guy alike, P.J. Clarke's offers a simple, classic dining experience.

The establishment has three distinct spaces. Enter through the bar, stepping past a small raw bar and over penny tiles as you pass into a small dining room before continuing into the main dining room. Red-and-white-checkered tablecloths cover each table. Those tables are packed on a weekday afternoon, a normal lunch crowd according to a waitress who calls me "Love" in a charming Irish accent. Old photographs and paintings cover the walls.

P.J. Clarke's served only men for a long time. Women could sidle up to a beer window and fill a bucket with booze before gaining entry in the 1960s. This window also came in handy during Prohibition.

The menu features classic American fare, including a selection of burgers. Among them: the standard Nat King Cole–approved cheeseburger, an organic turkey burger, and the Cadillac Burger, which pairs a slab of double smoked bacon with American cheese. But the best of the bunch is the Wild Mushroom Cheddar Burger; the beef and vegetables are smothered in a delectable whiskey onion sauce. The restaurant also serves plenty of seafood, including oysters, clams, shrimp, and lobster, a daily selection from the Fulton Fish Market.

The menu successfully straddles the line between classic and modern. For instance, its salad menu includes classic iceberg and Caesar salads but also offers a Chopped Kale and Avocado Salad with feta and walnuts that I doubt was available for the characters in *Mad Men* who dined here.

The dessert menu features the excellent apple and rhubarb cobbler. A large circular combination of warm fruit and biscuit, two generous scoops of vanilla ice cream top the dish and provide the perfect cooling agent. The ratio of ingredients is near perfect. Not too sweet and not too starchy, it's a winning exercise in flavor and texture. Other desserts include a cheesecake that comes with a side of blueberry compote and there's also a whiskey bread pudding (eat responsibly!).

P.J. Clarke's has expanded to several other locations: Lincoln Square and the financial district in Manhattan; Woodbury, New York; Washington, DC; and two locations in Sao Paulo, Brazil. But if you want to keep it as classic as possible, hit up the original location and get a real dose of old school New York.

THE PLAZA

768 5TH AVE, NEW YORK, NY 10019

(212) 759-3000 | FAIRMONT.COM

The smell of horses and extravagance greets your senses at the entrance to The Plaza. Located on Central Park South and 5th Avenue, it's luxury with a view. Capped doormen patrol the red-carpeted stairs at the entry. Five flags hang above. The American flag always waves on the far left. The Plaza Hotel flag always waves on the far right. The flags in between may change depending on who is at The Plaza or what event is being held here. On the fall day I visited, the management company's flag flapped in the breeze, as did the Saudi Arabian and Indian flags, honoring the nationalities of two Plaza owners.

Inside, the lobby awaits to the left. Stunning chandeliers hang from the high ceiling, and tables and couches provide seating in addition to a small bar. A man on the phone drops buzzwords like "equity" and "millions" into his cellphone. Well-accessorized women who look like they've had work done stroll through the elegant space. A second floor lobby overlooks the first and features plush red velvet couches, light fixtures shining purple beams, and chairs that look like they belong in a French chateau.

Straight ahead from the entrance, the first floor also features dining at the Palm Court. This space attempts to bring Central Park inside with palm trees and plants surrounding a circular bar and tables. It's the perfect atmosphere for afternoon tea or a bite to eat. The Palm Court is known for its kid-friendly menus, and you can count on seeing a child here enjoying an individual tower of desserts. Adults can choose from a wide array of cocktails or wines. Savory items like a caramelized butternut squash and apple soup or sweet items like a chocolate peanut tart provide hunger relief for more mature palates.

The original Plaza Hotel stood just seven stories high in 1890 and failed to impress New Yorkers. The U.S. Realty and Construction Company bought the hotel for $3 million in 1902 with funding from renowned gambler John W. Gates. Developers Bernhard Beinecke, Fred Sterry, and Harry S. Black joined forces to convert The Plaza into a grand display of luxury. They put $12.5 million into renovations with architect Henry Hardenbergh, whose credits beforehand included The Willard Hotel in Washington, DC and the original Waldorf Astoria. The group decided to model the hotel after a French castle. They installed 1,650 glass chandeliers and bought gold-encrusted china. No expense was spared. Their masterpiece opened to the public on October 1, 1907. Over half of the 800 rooms were designated as permanent residences for New York's richest. But wealthy guests could rent a room for $2.50.

Famous hotelier Conrad Hilton purchased the Plaza in 1943 for $7.4 million. He sold it to Donald Trump in 1988 for $390 million. Trump held on to The Plaza for seven years until he sold it at a loss for $325 million to Saudi Arabian Prince Al-Waleed Bin Talal. Al-Waleed hired Fairmont Hotels & Resorts to manage The Plaza. Al-Waleed's Kingdom Holdings, the Sahara Group, and the Elad Group own the hotel today. Fairmont continues to manage. As of this book's publication, the Sahara Group's founder Subrata Roy is incarcerated in India, so the Plaza's ownership may shift.

The Plaza has been designated a New York City Landmark and a National Historic Landmark. Many filmmakers have chosen The Plaza as a shooting location. Most famously, *The Great Gatsby*, *The Way We Were*, and the cinematic masterpiece, *Home Alone II: Lost In New York*, have all shot scenes at The Plaza.

The Plaza has played an important role in the children's book world as the home of Eloise in the book series *Eloise At The Plaza*. The books follow the misadventures of a little girl living in the hotel and inspired a movie of the same name starring Julie Andrews as her nanny. Author Kay Thompson lived at The Plaza, but some have theorized that Eloise is actually based on

her godmother, Liza Minnelli. The Plaza became a Literary Landmark in 1998 as a result of the popular book.

Today, the Plaza includes an Eloise store designed by kooky dressmaker Betsey Johnson. It smells like watermelon bubblegum and hosts tea parties for tots. An Eloise Suite, also designed by Johnson, is available for overnight stays. Its draws include a chandelier with pink lights, a zebra-print carpet, a sparkly pink bed, a tea set, and Eloise-themed dolls and apparel. The Edwardian Suite connects to this room for grown-ups who don't want to get lost in the pink. Like all suites, the Edwardian comes with a butler. Butlers at the Plaza can help with an array of tasks designed to anticipate or meet your needs, from unpacking your bags and drawing you a bath to shining your shoes and caring for dry cleaning.

The lower level of the Plaza includes a stunning food hall that outshines a shopping mall food court at every turn. Indoor benches are made to look as if they're outside in nature. Dining options include a noodle bar, bakery, lobster station, and pizzeria. Renowned chef Todd English paired with The Plaza to create his own Food Hall at The Plaza. His food hall has nine food stations offering a variety of cuisines. In addition to its lobby and food hall open to the public, The Plaza also features a number of shops. Merchandise includes books, clothing, jewelry, and handbags.

Staying at the Plaza promises luxury and beauty albeit for a hefty price, but New York natives or visitors alike should pop in to its public spaces for a free look at the historic landmark.

TAVERN ON THE GREEN

67 CENTRAL PARK WEST, NEW YORK, NY 10023

(212) 877-8684 | TAVERNONTHEGREEN.COM

> I felt my lungs inflate with the onrush of
> scenery—air, mountains, trees, people. I
> thought, "This is what it is to be happy."
> —*Sylvia Plath, The Bell Jar*

Central Park has long been an escape from the concrete jungle that dreams are made of in New York City. And for hungry souls inside its green acres, Tavern on the Green, located near the Sheep Meadow, provides food and beverage with a view.

In 1853 the state legislature authorized the City of New York to use public domain to appropriate more than 700 acres of land, running from 59th to 110th Streets north and south and from 5th to 8th (now Central Park West) Avenues spreading east to west and right in the center of Manhattan, for a huge public park. Its centralized location gave the project its succinct name: Central Park. The city held a landscape design competition for the park, and the "Greensward Plan" submitted by Frederick Law Olmsted and Calvert Vaux was the winner. They had been influenced by their mentor A. J. Downing, a landscape designer, considered the "Father of the American Park" because of his landscape plans of 1850 for the public grounds in Washington, DC. Downing advocated that cities throughout the United States provide recreational space for all citizens where they could escape the city's crowds and buildings without ever leaving the metropolis. A centrally located public space, Downing suggested, would become the "nucleus or heart of the village," demonstrating that nature and cities could co-exist.

In their winning design, Olmsted and Vaux anticipated that the entire island of Manhattan would eventually be developed like lower Manhattan, so they conceived a park environment that would be a natural oasis in the nation's busiest city to enhance the lives of all New Yorkers from all social backgrounds. In addition to the landscape of lawns, forests, bodies of water, rock elements, and paths that form the beautiful and often surprising landscape of Central Park, they created four cross-park roads for buses and cars that exist today. These are largely hidden out-of-sight to those in the park, accomplishing Olmstead and Vaux's goal of creating a green space removed from the hectic activity of the developing city. They also created three major paths that sometimes run parallel but never cross for pedestrians, horses, and carriages to get around the park (and that's the part that certainly has now changed).

When Central Park opened in 1857, Manhattan had been developed as far up as 59th Street, the southern boundary of the park. For the most part, the park was built on uninhabited swampy land, except for one particular section known as Seneca Village. This community stretched from 81st to 89th Streets between 7th and 8th Avenues and dates back to 1825, when many African American, Irish, and German families moved to this area. Around 1830, over half of the property owners in the area were African American. When the city bought this land in 1853 to build the park, 1,600 people were displaced, despite protests, and had to find new places to live.

Today, the park is central to all of Manhattan and accessible to anyone who cares to use it, but when it opened, because of its location in the northern undeveloped reaches of the island, it was most accessible to the rich who could get there in their carriages or using other transport, which New York's poorest citizens could not afford. Despite this anomaly, soon to change as New York's public transportation system developed, the park had many advantages for the disenfranchised who managed to get there.

The park provided a place for women to feel free in its early days. Living as second-class citizens without property or voting rights, women could not travel freely in the city without a chaperone. But Central Park and the Women's Pavilion there—now Summer Stage, home of Shakespeare in the Park—provided recreational space where women could socialize or exercise without their husbands, children, or chaperones. When bicycles came into vogue, many women were determined to learn to ride them, and to enjoy

an activity that gave them autonomy and got their hearts pumping and at a time when exercise wasn't considered ladylike. It was the same with ice-skating at Central Park's rink. In the park, women could do some cardio and even show off their ankles to prospective suitors (scandalous).

The park's design competition required a parade ground for the military to drill. So Olmstead and Vaux followed the rules and set aside a large grassy meadow for this purpose, The designers were convinced, however, that noisy military drills did not fit with the park's mission to provide a quiet escape from the city, and convinced the park commissioners that the grassy area should be turned over to a grazing place for sheep. So in 1864, a flock of 200 sheep was introduced to the large, grassy area on the west side of the park from 66th to 69th Streets. It became known as the Sheep Meadow.

The sheepfold or pen the city built to house the sheep was designed by Calvert Vaux and constructed in 1870. In 1934, the sheep got the boot finally and were sent first to Prospect Park in Brooklyn and eventually to the Catskills by Parks Commissioner Robert Moses. The sheepfold was converted into Tavern on the Green.

An article published in *The New York Times* before Tavern on the Green opened in 1934 announced that, "The Park Department promises that the Tavern on the Green will provide reasonably priced table d'hôte luncheon and dinner and á la carte service within reach of the average purse."

When Warner LeRoy took over in 1973, he transformed the restaurant into a luxurious dining destination well beyond the means of the "average purse." Central Park had deteriorated both physically and socially in the 1970s when the city was in terrible financial shape. The care of the park had been neglected; land and structures were eroding and crumbling, and frequent unsavory activity in the park made many reluctant to enter, and certainly not after dark. "This national treasure became a national disgrace," reports the official Central Park website.

The park's reputation hit an all-time low on April 19, 1989, with the assault of the Central Park jogger, a 28-year-old Wall Street investment banker, who was brutally beaten and raped while out for a run in the park. The story gripped the nation. The police arrested five teenage boys who'd been in the park that night. They all served jail time until the real criminal, Matias Reyes, came forward in 2002 and confessed that he alone had committed the assault and rape.

Since then, the park has become a much safer destination. A 1:00 a.m. curfew went into effect after the 1989 crime, and only seventeen robberies were reported in 2011, compared to 731 in 1981.

But LeRoy, a descendant of Hollywood royalty known for his shimmering ties of taffeta and velvet, had glitzed up Tavern on the Green and enticed New York's elite through the doors. He created the Crystal Room, a glass room filled with chandeliers, thus adding 400 seats to the restaurant.

John Lennon famously celebrated a birthday here, and plenty of famous guests visited the glamorous tavern, from Madonna and Michael Jackson to Yankee baseball players. The Crystal Room's addition technically violated municipal codes, but the city turned a blind eye because the restaurant needed the money that the expansion would bring in from additional room for more customers. When the city hired urban planner Elizabeth Barlow as its Central Park Administrator in 1979, she turned around the conditions in the park. Today, the park has been restored to its former glory as a safe and beautiful refuge within the city.

Tavern on the Green served 1,500 guests a day at its height, and it consistently was among the top earning restaurants in the country. In 2007, the restaurant reported $37.6 million in revenues to earn the second-place spot in the country. It held the number two spot in 2009, but its revenue dropped to $27 million. The 2008 recession took an irreversible toll on the restaurant. About 60 percent of the restaurant's business came from banquets and corporate events. Pricy events at Tavern on the Green were the types of expenses cash-strapped New York businesses eliminated, and this hit the tavern's profits significantly. The New York City Parks Department declined to renew LeRoy's lease in 2009. The restaurant filed for bankruptcy in September of 2009 and closed on the last day of the year.

The city entertained bids from new proprietors, even one from Donald Trump, who promised that Tavern on the Green would be "the highest-grossing restaurant on the planet" under his direction. But David Salama and Jim Caiola were the winners, and the decision was controversial. Although they were relatively inexperienced—they owned a crêpe restaurant in Philadelphia—Salama and Caiola had a personal connection to Mayor Bloomberg's office that put them over the top. The *New York Post* channeled public sentiment about the decision into a headline: "What A Load of Crêpe!" The new Tavern on the Green opened in 2014 to negative reviews. *The New York Times* put it best: "Is it too late to bring back the sheep?"

Two years later, I lunched at Tavern on The Green on a beautiful fall day. The menu is ambitious, and while it does not hit every note, along with the decor and location it hits enough to justify the high bill that is definitely beyond "the average purse." You can expect to pay between $50 and $100 per person to eat where sheep were once housed.

Starters range from oysters á la carte and steak tartare to salads and risotto. The chopped salad is made with many tasty ingredients like pear, gorgonzola, and walnuts, but it was drenched with so much dressing that it was difficult to identify and appreciate all the individual elements. Soft, creamy buratta is a winning dish accompanied by squash with a pomegranate dressing and fresh basil. It's a delicious starter with a pleasing mix of textures.

Main courses range from coq au vin and salmon to roasted rack of lamb and duck confit. The hamburger is made from short rib and brisket. Dense and large, it's a filling dish. The salt and vinegar chips that come with the burger are drenched in too much salt. The all-day bar menu includes items from $9 to $24, such as a pickle plate, a cheese plate, clams casino, and roasted figs.

The restaurant also offers a "Green to Go" menu, perfect for carting to Sheep Meadow for a picnic. This menu offers sandwiches that start at around $10, breakfast items like yogurt and muffins, and a variety of snacks to grab and go.

Desserts from pastry chef Ryan Witcher vary and delight. The dessert menu's top seller is the espresso crème brûlée. The chocolate-hazelnut biscotti that tops the dish, however, is nothing to write home about. The carrot cake also sells well, with caramelized pineapple on top of cream cheese icing. The warm apple crisp is terrific, a winning combination of warm diced apples, cold vanilla ice cream, and toasted coconut streusel, a delight to the palette. The presentation in a two-tiered dish, which resembles a fishbowl, makes the dish even more enjoyable.

The location of the restaurant inside Central Park, with views of the Sheep Meadow and the passing horse-drawn carriages, is hard to beat, and the restaurant's glamorous design makes for an appealing visual experience. The restaurant has several distinct seating areas, each with a unique atmosphere. Unfortunately, the food does not match the stunning surroundings in which it is served.

The arched entrance to the restaurant is through double doors protected by a long red awning. Customers can eat in the lobby seated on a plush red sofa or drink at the handsome circular bar with its attractive leather barstools or comfortable paisley couches. There's a choice of dining rooms. one drenched in light from large windows and decorated in beige tones, and another darker room with wood details and high ceilings. Outside in the garden, diners can eat under umbrellas and circus-tent shaped lights. The beer garden is another outdoor dining space with seating at upscale picnic tables shaded by umbrellas.

Despite its ups and downs, Tavern on the Green in Central Park continues to attract people. In 2015, it ranked ninety-three in the nation's top grossing restaurants with $12.3 million in sales, a far cry from its successful days before the 2008 recession. Nonetheless, there is, quite possibly, no better place to which your brain might lead you to dine than a glamorous restaurant with gorgeous views in a beautiful park. So, Tavern on the Green should be around for a long time, and it is worth a visit.

WALDORF ASTORIA NEW YORK

301 PARK AVE, NEW YORK, NY 10022

(212) 355-3000 | WWW.WALDORFNEWYORK.COM

A rivalry between cousins paved the way for one of New York's oldest and most lavish hotels. William Waldorf Astor and John Jacob Astor IV were both great-grandsons of the famous John Jacob Astor. Astor made a fortune in the fur trade and as a real estate mogul. At the time of his death in 1848, the German immigrant was the richest man in the country with an estate worth about $20 million. His great-grandsons despised one another, and their rivalry played out in the hotel business.

Before moving to England, William built a thirteen-story hotel next to John's four-story mansion on Fifth Avenue and 33rd Street to annoy his cousin. Before the hotel's March opening in 1893, *The New York Times* described the Waldorf Hotel as a palace. Designed by Henry Hardenbergh, it cost $3 million, with $800,000 alone spent on interior decoration. One of the rooms boasted a $3,500 bed that replicated the bed that King Francis I of France slept in during the early sixteenth century. The ladies' drawing room copied Marie Antoinette's apartment.

Not to be outdone, John built his own hotel right next door to the Waldorf in 1897. He made sure it stood taller than his cousin's hotel by building it seventeen stories tall and aimed to outdo The Waldorf in design. He named his venture the Astoria Hotel after his grandfather's fur trading post on the west coast. Reporting on the Astoria Hotel's opening in 1897, *The New York Times* raved that the building "seems to be as complete and magnificent as modern workmen and modern art can make it." The newspaper praised the Astoria's "creations in decorative and upholstering skill that probably have not their equal in the world." The Astor Gallery even replicated the Hall of Mirrors in Versailles.

Both cousins had built state-of-the-art hotels. They eventually decided to put aside their differences and unite the hotels as the Waldorf Astoria Hotel. They connected their establishments with a 300-foot-long marble hallway. This simple connection could be easily sealed should their partnership turn sour, a threat they each made. This corridor earned the name Peacock Hallway because common people often watched the parade of wealthy patrons strutting like peacocks putting on a show between the two buildings.

The Waldorf Astoria revolutionized the hospitality industry by being the first hotel to offer private bathrooms, room service, and a menu for kids. Oscar Tschirky, the Waldorf Astoria's maître d'hotel from 1893 to 1943, also boosted the Waldorf Astoria's penchant for innovation by inventing the Waldorf Salad and popularizing Thousand Island dressing while in the

hotel's employ. The salad originally combined chopped apples and celery in mayonnaise. It has been updated to include walnuts and grapes, and chefs now usually swap out mayonnaise in favor of yogurt and/or crème fraiche. When Oscar died in 1950 the Waldorf Astoria lowered all its flags to half-mast.

After John died on the *Titanic* in 1912 and William passed away in 1919, their hotel began to struggle. The hotel had a hard time competing with more modern hotels emerging in the 1920s. Prohibition certainly hindered the hotel's moneymaking nightlife. Developers purchased the hotel from Lucius Boomer, the new owner, in 1929 for $13.5 million to construct the Empire State Building in its place.

But Boomer purchased the rights to the name "Waldorf Astoria" for a dollar and decided to open a new version of the hotel uptown on Park Avenue stretching from 49th to 50th streets. The forty-seven-story hotel opened its doors on October 1, 1931, and continues to operate today. It has a secret and private train platform, reached from a locked door on East 49th Street, called Track 61 connecting it to Grand Central Terminal. President Franklin D. Roosevelt used it when he visited the Waldorf Astoria in part to lower the visibility of his disability from polio. (*The Amazing Spider Man 2* used Track 61 as inspiration for a secret subway station named Roosevelt in the film.) Boomer honored the original Waldorf Astoria by naming one of the lounges Peacock Alley and by placing a nine-foot-tall bronze antique clock from the earlier hotel in the new lobby.

The Waldorf Astoria features luxurious rooms and apartments for long-term stays on its top fifteen floors. Marilyn Monroe lived in a suite at the Waldorf Astoria in 1955. Herbert Hoover lived there after he left the White House from 1933 to 1964. And Dwight Eisenhower lived in the hotel from 1967 to 1969.

Like Roosevelt, every president from Hoover to Obama has stayed at the Waldorf Astoria in the Presidential Suite. This suite has many rooms to accommodate presidential staff as well as bulletproof windows, and

mementos are left behind as a tradition by each president. In addition, the suite has accommodated royalty and heads of state from other countries, including Queen Elizabeth II of England, King Hussein of Jordan, Prime Minister David Ben-Gurion of Israel, and Emperor and Empress Hirohito of Japan.

Hotelier Conrad Hilton long admired the Waldorf Astoria. When it opened in 1931, he wrote "The Greatest of Them All" on a newspaper photo of the hotel. Almost two decades later in 1949, he took over the management of the Waldorf Astoria, and in 1972, he bought the property. It changed hands again in 2014 when Hilton sold the hotel to the Chinese company Anbang Insurance Group for $1.95 billion.

Typically, U.S. heads of state have stayed at the Waldorf when attending the opening of the United Nations General Assembly in the fall. But in 2015, the seventieth anniversary of the United Nations, President Obama and his team were concerned that the Chinese-owned hotel might be bugged. So the president stayed instead at the South Korean–owned Lotte New York Palace Hotel.

The Waldorf Astoria features a number of dining options. The Bull & Bear Steakhouse features seafood and black angus beef that has been wet-aged for twenty-eight days. La Chine fuses Chinese and French flavors. The menu begins with a quote from famous culinary columnist and TV personality James Beard: "In all the world there are only really two great cuisines: The Chinese and the French." Your taste buds will have to test his theory. And Peacock Alley serves lunch and small plates like sliders, charcuterie, risotto balls, and cocktails until 1 a.m. on Fridays and Saturdays. The hotel has two other bars as well: Bull & Bear Bar and Sir Harry's. The Bull & Bear Bar features stock market-inspired decor, including a ticker-tape machine. Sir Harry's takes its name from the British explorer Sir Harry Hamilton Johnston.

The Waldorf Astoria became a New York City Landmark in 1993. Head for this New York institution to rest your head, enjoy a meal, or revel in architectural beauty, but if you are harboring a secret, you might consider President Obama's move.

WHITE HORSE TAVERN

567 HUDSON STREET, NEW YORK, NY 10014

(212) 989-3956

I wish people were as excited about seeing writers work in public as they used to be. Alas, today's Starbucks screenwriters are more likely to receive complimentary eye rolls than star-struck smiles. Unlike today's Buzzfeed Quiz authors, young writers in the 1950s were revered. The average citizen could recite poetry from memory. In the 1950s, as the nation grappled with conflicting social movements (*Playboy* versus *Leave It To Beaver*), a generation of poets rose to prominence. They wanted to bring poetry out of the classroom and "back to the streets" with unstructured immediacy. They valued drugs, sex, Zen Buddhism, and jazz. They were known as the Beat poets, and they hung out in New York on Hudson Street at the White Horse Tavern.

This Greenwich Village tavern has been pouring drinks since 1880. The bar originally attracted longshoremen who earned their keep at the nearby Hudson River piers. In the mid-twentieth century it became a popular hangout for writers and musicians.

The White Horse Tavern is a long space divided into three rooms: a front bar and two dining rooms. It feels old and cramped. On theme, white horses neigh from every room in pictures or statues. A chandelier featuring several white horses hangs by the bar. A long sidewalk cafe outside attracts large crowds.

A peculiar sign above the bar reads: "Proper ID Proving 25 Years of Age Required." A bartender who's been here for two decades explains, "We don't like people under twenty-five." So, drunk 21- and 22-year olds: Make other arrangements. The bar tends to enforce the rule at night. The bar has remained consistent, as the neighborhood has transformed from a working class area to a ritzy neighborhood over the years.

The West Village has always attracted artists. William Dunlap, known as the father of the American theatre, lived in Greenwich Village in the eighteenth century. So did Thomas Paine, author of *Common Sense*, the pamphlet that inspired many to join the Patriot cause of the American Revolution. Edgar Allen Poe, Mark Twain, and *The New York Times* founder Henry Jarvis Raymond all called the Village home. Author John Strausbaugh, who penned *The Village: 400 Years of Beats and Bohemians, Radicals and Rogues*, argues that the Village's location and deviation from the grid system made it an oddball, non-central location that attracted the people who weren't in New York City to line their pockets. The close proximity to New York University also infused the neighborhood with thinkers. Because the streets in this neighborhood are also shorter and closer together, geography promoted collaboration. Not only did artists move to this area, but they were literally on top of one another, which made for great opportunities to collaborate or influence one another.

One place for these artists to come together was the White Horse Tavern, which united many of New York's working class writers. The best known of the Beats were Allen Ginsberg and Jack Kerouac. Kerouac reportedly devised the Beats' nickname because it encapsulated how he and his peers felt: beat down. Kerouac's rowdy behavior earned him eviction from the bar on several occasions, and "Go home, Kerouac" was once scrawled above the back of a urinal. Other writers that have quenched their thirst at the White Horse Tavern include John Ashbery (*Some Trees, Self-Portrait in a Convex Mirror*), Hunter S. Thompson (*Fear and Loathing in Las Vegas*), Frank O'Hara (*Lunch Poems*), Norman Mailer (*The Naked and the Dead*), and James Baldwin (*Go Tell It on the Mountain*).

But the writer most associated with the White Horse Tavern is Dylan Thomas. The Welsh poet, known as the "modern Keats," reportedly liked this bar because it reminded him of the bars in Wales. He famously downed eighteen whiskies here on November 9, 1953, returned to the Chelsea Hotel, collapsed, and died that night at St. Vincent Hospital. He was 39.

Thomas hailed from South Wales. His first poem was published in a magazine when he was 17, and his first collection of poetry was published just three years later. He explored themes of love, deterioration, and loneliness, among others. As he aged, his work became increasingly accessible to the average reader. For instance, the poem he's best known for—"Do Not Go Gentle into That Goodnight"—is much easier to comprehend than his earlier work. Most believe the poem to be about the death of Thomas's father, but he reportedly told his friend Robert J. Gibson that he wrote the poem about his father's loss of sight (but readers, he insisted, should interpret it as they wish). A giant painting of Thomas hangs in the tavern's second room.

The other defining poem of the Beats is most certainly Alan Ginsberg's *Howl*. Published in the 1956 book, *Howl and Other Poems*, by Lawrence Ferlinghetti's City Lights Books, the book incited uproar for its sexual content. The poem begins with the famous lines, "I saw the best minds of my generation destroyed by madness, starving hysterical naked, dragging themselves

through the negro streets at dawn looking for an angry fix." It goes on to celebrate sex and homosexuality with descriptions of "torsos night after night with dreams, with drugs, with waking nightmares, alcohol and cock and endless balls." It describes men "who let themselves be fucked in the ass by saintly motorcyclists" and "scatter[ed] their semen freely to whomever come who may." Ginsberg described others who "sweetened the snatches of a million girls trembling in the sunset."

The publisher had anticipated negative reactions to Ginsberg's work. He even had copies printed in England and shipped to San Francisco to avoid pre-production roadblocks. Once in the United States, those roadblocks reared their heads. U.S. Customs seized 520 copies of the book in March of 1957. Three months later, undercover cops bought copies at San Francisco's City Lights Bookstore and then arrested Ferlinghetti for publishing obscene material. The case went to court and Judge Clayton W. Horn ultimately ruled that the book was not obscene. Ginsberg and the Beats were part of a larger group of artists that challenged the status quo and paved the way for the countercultural movements and political upheaval of the 1960s.

Greenwich Village has changed dramatically since the 1960s. Rents and local prices in restaurants and bars have progressively become impassively expensive. The 1980s AIDS crisis literally killed off many of the Village's residents. Today's Greenwich Village looks somewhat the same as in its bohemian heyday, but the price tag has changed.

Despite the influx of wealthy locals, the White Horse Tavern retains its working class vibe. Slightly run down, its cash-only menu features standard pub fare like potato skins and chili along with burgers, sandwiches—most notably, an excellent grilled cheese—and a brunch menu of eggs, French toast, and pancakes. And as far as alcohol goes, if you order whiskey, please stay well below eighteen shots.

BROOKLYN

BAMONTE'S

32 WITHERS ST, BROOKLYN, NY 11211

(718) 384-8831

In the television series *Master of None* from Aziz Ansari, Ansari's alter ego, Dev, helps his girlfriend's grandmother sneak out of her old folks home. With her few hours of freedom, she has one destination in mind: Bamonte's.

This old school Italian restaurant in Williamsburg has been making marinara since 1900. Its unassuming exterior gives way to a much more upscale, old school interior. Romantic drapes adorn the windows and white tablecloths cover the tables. Paintings hang in golden frames and busts decorate the purple and taupe walls. A giant, ornate chandelier hanging in the center of the dining room looks straight out of *Beauty and the Beast*. Servers take orders dressed in jackets and bowties.

Founder Pasquale Bamonte Sr. made pianos in Salerno, a southwestern city and province of Italy. But America beckoned. So Pasquale, his wife Rose, and their children packed their bags and moved from Italy to Williamsburg, Brooklyn, in the late nineteenth century. Pasquale originally found work as a carpenter and then bought the property that would one day become Bamonte's in 1900. He and Rose operated it as a banquet hall named Liberty Hall to start, hosting weddings, society meetings, and other celebrations. It evolved into a restaurant named Bamonte's and has been run by his family ever since.

Pasquale's son, Pasquale Jr., took over the operation with his brother John. After Pasquale Jr.'s death, his wife, Filomena, ran the restaurant with John, who eventually bought Filomena out for full ownership. After John passed away, his nephew Anthony (Filomena and Pasquale Jr.'s son) assumed control.

Anthony grew up working in the kitchen at Bamonte's, and he runs the business today with his three daughters Nicole, Laura, and Lisa. Like their father, these women began working at Bamonte's in high school. "If you want to go into this business," counsels Anthony, "take the handles off the clock." It seems that for four generations the Bamonte family has had no idea what time it is.

The menu features classic Italian fare with an emphasis on Neapolitan cuisine. (Naples is only about an hour's drive from the Bamontes' hometown of Salerno.) The coastal city commonly features pastas that contain seafood, and so does Bamonte's, such as the popular linguine with white clam sauce. The menu also features plenty of stand-alone seafood dishes like the Seafodo Fra Diavolo (shrimps, clams, mussels, and calamari in spicy tomato sauce), broiled lobster tails, and monkfish oreganata (with oregano-infused breadcrumbs). But the most popular dish of all is the gigantic pork chop sautéed with a mix of hot and sweet peppers. All sauces and desserts are made in house, and the kitchen uses pastas and olive oil imported from Italy.

The menu has evolved over the years. Nicole describes the original menu as "peasant food." She elaborates, "Years ago they used to put pigs ears on the [menu.] . . . Anything that they were able to get, that's what they would serve." As a successful restaurant, the kitchen can be more discerning today. You won't find pigs ears on anyone's plate. You will find classic dishes that have worked for decades. "It's plain and simple food," says Anthony. Nicole adds: "People feel like they're at home or their grandmother's house."

Bamonte's was a popular hangout for Italian Americans in the Italian American Democratic League and for Italian American baseball players like Joe DiMaggio, Carl Furillo, and Tommy Lasorda.

In addition to Netflix's *Master of None*, several other productions have filmed at Bamonte's, including *Gotham*, *Person of Interest*, and *The Sopranos*. The restaurant's parking lot makes setting up film equipment here relatively easy. It also expands Bamonte's customer base to drivers from Connecticut and Long Island.

Bamonte's upscale family atmosphere offers travelers near and far a pleasant meal at a Williamsburg staple.

FERDINANDO'S FOCACCERIA

151 UNION ST, BROOKLYN, NY 11231

(718) 855-1545

Head for Ferdinando's Focacceria in Cobble Hill, Brooklyn, for authentic Sicilian food. Since 1904, this restaurant has been serving up dishes like spleen sandwiches, rice balls, and ricotta-topped fried chickpeas. The establishment originally opened as Paul's Focacceria when Paul Benfante managed it. Longshoremen from the nearby piers comprised about ninety-five percent of the restaurant's clientele back then.

When Paul's Focacceria opened in the early twentieth century, Italian immigrants faced considerable discrimination throughout the country. Before 1880, most of America's Italian immigrants were skilled laborers from the north. But a population increase and an economic crash in Southern Italy sent hoards of uneducated, unskilled Southern Italians to the United States post-1880. As *The New York Times* put it in an article from 1882, "There has never been since New York was founded so low and ignorant a class among the immigrants who poured in here as the Southern Italians who have been crowding our docks during the past year."

Anti-Italianism appeared to stem from several sources. First, Italians were seen as lawless. American journalists reported on the high rates of crime in Italy, contributing to the lawless stereotype formed in many American minds regarding Italian immigrants. Even today, organized crime is intrinsically linked with Italian American families. Second, their unfamiliar features and dark skin led to mistreatment. Until the 1880s, most immigrants hailed from Western Europe, so the atypical features of Southern and Eastern Europeans motivated racism. And third, Italian immigrants' Catholic faith yielded discrimination in a heavily Protestant nation.

The largest mass lynching on record in American history took place in New Orleans in 1891. The victims were a group of Italians who'd been found not guilty of murdering a police chief. People who disagreed with the verdict lynched the nine defendants, plus two other Italian immigrants. John Parker, one of the men who organized the lynching, became governor of Louisiana. In 1911, he characterized Italians as "just a little worse than the Negro, being if anything filthier in [their] habits, lawless, and treacherous." Future President Teddy Roosevelt called the lynchings "a rather good thing."

World War I and World War II helped change the American perception of Italian immigrants, particularly as Italians served in the army, and also because American soldiers spent time abroad and gained an appreciation for Italian culture. New York City even elected Italian-American Fiorello La Guardia to the mayor's office for three terms from 1934 to 1945.

Ferdinando's second owner, Ferdinando Ciaramitaro, worked as a cook in the Italian Navy before Benfante offered him a job, and he moved to New York with his family. He eventually took over the restaurant. Ferdinando died in 1975, and his son-in-law Francesco (Frank) Buffa took the reigns. Buffa remains at the helm today.

Buffa immigrated to New York from Italy in 1971 at age 21. Sicilian born, he worked as a police officer in Rome for three years before moving to New

York. "I had zero knowledge of the food business," he recalls. He had been studying to become a physical therapist in Rome in his off-hours working as a cop. But Buffa met Ferdinando's daughter in Brooklyn, they married, and Buffa took over the restaurant. Before he passed away in 1975, Ferdinando passed his recipes as well as his business to Buffa. "He treated me like his own son," reflects Buffa. Under Buffa's direction, the restaurant expanded from a lunch spot to a dinner destination and added more Sicilian items to the menu. Originally the menu offered only three items: a spleen sandwich, a fried chickpea sandwich, and potato croquettes. They remain central and popular items on the menu.

Ferdinando's most famous draw is the spleen sandwich. Called a *vastedda*, this sandwich marries a cow spleen with fluffy ricotta and grated caciocavella cheeses. Buffa says that *vastedda* was best known as a food for the poor in Sicily. In an article on the spleen sandwich for *The Atlantic*, Tejal Rao described the spleen as follows: "Spleen tastes like the broiled, grizzly flotsam of a prehistoric monster. Like a fictional creature butchered and left to rot in an ogre's cellar."

With that endorsement, I bit into my *vestedda* with great trepidation. I was pleasantly surprised that nothing bit me back. No monster lay within this homemade roll. Tough and strange, *vastedda* is an acquired taste. But, as my waitress put it, for $6.50 a sandwich, it's not a big loss if you hate it. And if you love it, what a bargain! On a Tuesday afternoon in late October, one customer told me that she comes all the way from New Jersey to eat *vastedda* at Ferdinando's.

The less challenging *panelle* pairs fried chickpeas with ricotta and caciocavello cheeses. This sandwich tastes understated, as do the potato croquettes. But the *arancina* (rice ball) is the best dish on the menu, familiar enough to those craving Italian cuisine, but distinct enough for those seeking something new. A giant ball of rice laced with specks of beef and peas, an arancina is rolled in breadcrumbs, fried, and served with marinara sauce and cheese. Fernando's version is delicious.

The menu also features hot and cold antipasto, including fried shrimp and squid, stuffed sundried tomatoes, and stuffed artichokes. Entrees include Italian classics such as penne arrabbiata and chicken parmigiana. Homemade cannolis are a sweet after-dinner treat.

The atmosphere evokes Sicilian culture. Buffa has decorated the walls with maps of Italy and photos of Buffa's native Carini. Framed photos of Buffa with his son David and famous visitors like Leonardi DiCaprio and Pierce Brosnan hang near the entrance.

If your taste buds have been asking for a new adventure, head to Ferdinando's Focacceria and try the *vastedda*. This joint has been preparing tasty Sicilian options that are difficult to find anywhere else for over a century.

MONTE'S

451 CARROLL ST, BROOKLYN, NY 11215

(718) 852-7800 | MONTESNYC.COM

If you want a little piece of Venice, head to Gowanus, Brooklyn. You'll have to stretch your imagination, but if you don't wear your glasses, the fuzzy Gowanus Canal just might harken images of Venice's romantic, gondola-filled canals. Steps from the 1.8-mile canal, park your gondola at Monte's. At 110, it's Brooklyn's oldest Italian restaurant.

Angelo and Filomena Montemarano opened this restaurant in 1906 under the name, Angelo's Tavern. The husband and wife lived upstairs with their children. Their son Nick eventually took over the operation. Nick Montemarano transformed Angelo's Tavern into an upscale eatery favored by the Rat Pack and the Mob. After visiting Venice, Nick renamed the restaurant Monte's Venetian Room in 1938. He redecorated the space with a wraparound Venetian mural, and some patrons even traveled to the restaurant by boat.

During Prohibition, Monte's stayed in business as a speakeasy and even manufactured its own beer. In the event of a police raid, employees threw booze through a chute into the basement. This chute has since been sealed.

The Rat Pack socialized here. Frank Sinatra favored the Italian ricotta cheesecake. Sammy Davis Jr. once gave a surprise concert here. And movies like *Prizzi's Honor* and *Men of Respect* have used Monte's as a shooting location.

It took a while for the Gowanus Canal to reach its current level of environmental distress. The area was originally a marsh rich with huge oysters. Dutch settlers named the marsh after Chief Gouwane of the Canarsee Native American tribe. Dutch settlers exported barrels of Gowanus oysters to Europe in the 1600s. During the American Revolution's battles of

Brooklyn and Long Island, the marsh slowed down British forces that chose not to follow American troops through the wetlands. Then in 1848, the city built the Gowanus Canal to connect the area to the Red Hook Port. The canal became an important commercial passageway. In the 1860s, barges transported coal, timber, sand, and the brownstone that would be used to build many of New York's homes up the canal. The neighborhood became an industrial hotspot full of factories. Those factories pumped pollutants into the Gowanus Canal.

By the early twentieth century, an alarming amount of sewage filled the canal. In 1911, the city began pumping fresh seawater into the canal. But the pump broke in 1961 and wasn't fixed again until 1999. The canal hosts many diseases and the occasional dead body (thanks to Mafia drops). Its nicknames include "Perfume Creek" and "Lavender Lake." Locals joke that if you use a bathroom in Carroll Gardens, you can run downstream with the canal and see your own waste. *The New York Times* wrote about the canal in 1998: "The smell is less a scent than an assault that reaches in to choke the throat." I'm happy to report that when I crossed the canal in November of 2015, I did not detect much in the way of an odor, and my nose remains intact. The Environmental Protection Agency (EPA) declared the Gowanus Canal a Superfund site in 2010, and a $506 million cleanup should start in 2017.

The Gowanus neighborhood, bordered by Carroll Gardens to the west, Park Slope to the east, and Boerum Hill to the north, has evolved dramatically in recent years. Like many neighborhoods, developers have come in, and the price of real estate has soared. Monte's current co-owner, Dominick Castlevetre, grew up in the neighborhood when Italians dominated. "Everybody was a cousin [or] related somehow," he says. Castlevetre grew up four doors from Monte's and worked as a valet for the restaurant in his teenage years. The restaurant closed in 2007 when Nick passed away. Castlevetre and his wife, Tina Esposito, stepped in to revive the restaurant in 2011.

Castlevetre worked as a pizza maker with his father-in-law. He has put those skills to use again with a superb pizza menu, incorporating offerings from classic margherita to a prosciutto and arugula pie. But the *bresaola* pizza—a combination of mozzarella, mushrooms, baby spinach, parmigiano, truffle oil, and air-dried beef—reigns supreme. *Bresaola* is an air-dried beef that has been aged for a few months until it resembles, essentially, a fruit roll-up. Thin, salty, and purple, it's the perfect topping for any meat lover.

Monte's makes its own pasta and imports olive oil from Italy. Pasta dishes include spinach gnocchi in a walnut-gorgonzola sauce and garganelli

with roasted duck ragu. The menu also features plenty of meat and sea-food dishes, from salmon to lamb chops and sirloin steak. The braised short ribs stand out; they are tender after cooking for hours in a fantastic red wine sauce. The dessert menu features classic Italian sweets like tira-misu and tartufo while also offering a Nutella calzone and a Nutella and strawberry pizza. If you can't make it in to the restaurant, enjoy the menu from the comfort of your home. Delivery orders make up about 20 percent of Monte's business.

Monte's offers a romantic atmosphere off the beaten path. Tucked between the F and R subway stations, the restaurant is easily accessible but somewhat hidden off the main streets. Candles in mason jars light every table. Your pupils will dilate in the dark space while you stare into your date's eyes or at a beautiful pizza. The walls no longer directly conjure images of Venice, but now pay tribute to the neighborhood with a collec-tion of area maps. As the neighborhood has changed and will undoubtedly continue to change, head to Monte's and enjoy a night at a restaurant that has seen and survived it all.

NATHAN'S FAMOUS

1310 SURF AVENUE, BROOKLYN, NY 11224

(718) 333-2202 | NATHANSFAMOUS.COM

Americans eat 450 hot dogs a second. The tubular sausage swaddled in a soft bun is as American as baseball. And in true American fashion, hot dogs came to this country courtesy of immigrants in the nineteenth century. The popularity of hot dogs has soared from sea to shining sea, and one Coney Island business deserves credit: Nathan's Famous.

Hot dog historians (best job ever?) have identified references to hot dogs as early as the 9th century B.C. in Homer's masterpiece, *The Odyssey*: "These goat sausages sizzling here in the fire—we packed them with fat and blood to have for supper. Now, whoever wins this bout and proves the stronger, let that man step up and take his pick of the lot!" Frankfurt, Germany, and Vienna, Austria, both lay claim to the modern hot dog, or, rather *frankfurter* or *weiner*. When German and Austrian immigrants came to the United States, so did hot dogs. One of those immigrants was Charles Feltman. He launched a pushcart operation selling hot dogs in Brooklyn in 1867. Beachgoers liked the ease of eating a sausage without utensils or plates (plus, it generated no garbage). Feltman built his business into a large, upscale restaurant complex complete with its own carousel called Feltman's. There, he sold hot dogs, or Coney Island red hots, as he relabeled them, for ten cents apiece. But one of his employees, Nathan Handwerker, would steal his thunder.

Nathan was born in Poland in 1892. He was one of thirteen children. The family had very little money, so at age eleven his parents sent him to live and work in a bakery. He slept on a cot in the bakery's kitchen, rising early to make dough and hawk knishes in the streets. After two years, lonesome Nathan wanted to return to his parents. He took the money he'd saved and

went to a butcher shop. He returned home to his parents and siblings with a sack full of meat. (If your modern teenager is acting out, read them this paragraph.)

As World War I approached, Nathan set his sights on America. Worried that packing his belongings in a suitcase would arouse police suspicion as to why he wasn't serving in the army as he should have been, Nathan put his underwear and one pair of pants in an onion bag. He successfully made it to Belgium without incident. He worked there until he had enough money saved for passage to the United States. He arrived at Ellis Island in 1912. He couldn't speak English. He could barely even read or write in Polish. But he had something more important: hustle.

Nathan worked at a bakery and then at Feltman's with entertainers Jimmy Durante and Eddie Cantor before they hit it big. Durante and Cantor complained that Feltman's hot dogs cost too much at ten cents apiece. Nathan saw an opportunity.

In 1916, Nathan and his wife, Ida, opened their own hot dog stand and christened it Nathan's Famous. Their strategy? Cut Feltman's price in half. For five cents, hungry beach goers could gobble a hot dog whose recipe came to America via Ida's grandmother.

But Nathan's cheap prices didn't immediately drive customers in the door. Suspicious of such a good deal, potential customers shied away, reasoning that the meat must be terribly low quality. Rumors about the unsavory contents of hot dogs (is it dog meat?) didn't help. So Nathan and Ida got creative. They hired actors to don white coats and eat their product outside. If doctors ate hot dogs, they must be all right! The scheme worked. Also helping business, the city finished construction on the subway from Manhattan to Coney Island in 1920. A whole new customer base could now reach Nathan's. For five cents, Manhattanites could ride the subway to the beach, where another five cents got them a hot dog from Nathan's Famous, coining Coney Island the "Nickel Empire."

The subway cemented Coney Island as a fun, kitschy escape for sun-starved city dwellers. The beach town already had an amusement park at the turn of the century, but in 1920 the Wonder Wheel opened, followed by the boardwalk in 1923, and The Cyclone rollercoaster in 1927. Coney Island became known as a weird, fun, and sexual place to enjoy in the summertime. The Mermaid Parade that has kicked off the summer season since 1985 embodies this reputation. It feels like a mash up of the Gay Pride Parade and *The Little Mermaid*.

While exploring Coney Island, you will probably see a somewhat disturbing face with a wide, off-putting grin plastered everywhere. The unofficial logo of Coney Island, this "funny face" was the original mascot of an amusement park called the Steeplechase Park, where women entering the park were treated to gusts of wind that blew their skirts up, and a dwarf dressed like a clown pursued patrons with an electric paddle. The creepy logo embodied this sexualized adventure park.

In its early days, Nathan's was a fast-paced, greasy hotspot pulsing with energy and, at times, a tough vibe. Drunks showed up late at night, and the occasional fight broke out. It was the kind of place where celebrities like Jackie Kennedy Onassis went to "slum it." She even had Nathan's hot dogs served at the White House. Nathan's Famous was so popular that Nathan's put the police on its payroll to turn a blind eye when customers double parked outside to run in and grab an order.

Nathan and Ida enjoyed local success for about four decades. Contrary to what some people may believe, Nathan's didn't run Feltman's out of business. Feltman's did close in 1954, but only after the businesses co-existed for four decades. As Feltman's closed its doors, Nathan's started to expand beyond Coney Island.

Expansion caused squabbles between Nathan and his two sons, Murray and Sol. Sol's grandson Lloyd Handwerker explores the internal conflict in his documentary *Famous Nathan*, which played at the Tribeca Film Festival in 2014. Sol broke away from the family business and opened his own restaurant called Snack Time in 1963. The Midtown Manhattan restaurant sold hot dogs, hamburgers, and seafood—a similar menu to Nathan's. Sol even advertised that he was Nathan's son as a selling point. But he never worked for Nathan's again.

Quite the opposite, Murray teamed with his father to expand Nathan's with franchises in other states. Murray spearheaded the effort to take Nathan's public in 1968. As Murray grew the company, his father struggled in retirement. Accustomed to hard work his whole life, he found the languid pace of retirement boring. Nathan passed away in 1974 at age 81. His employees lined up along Surf Avenue with their hands over their hearts as his hearse passed.

In 1971 Nathan's stock was priced at $42. But a decade later, it had dropped to $1. Murray sold the struggling business to the Equicor Group in 1987. It remained private for six years but went public once again in 1993. The new owners focused on smaller operations within highly trafficked areas like stadiums, airports, department stores, and malls. They also added supermarket retail to the operation. Today, 238 Nathan's restaurants operate nationwide, and the company has outposts in Kuwait, Russia, the Dominican Republic, Jamaica, Mexico, Egypt, Costa Rica, and Turkey.

Of course, the event that makes Nathan's a trending topic every year is the infamous Hot Dog Eating Contest held on Coney Island each July 4th. The story goes that Nathan and Ida hosted the first contest in 1916 between four immigrants. Whoever ate the most hot dogs could claim he loved America the most. Because even a century ago, people knew gluttony was the fastest way to assimilate.

The contest has grown in popularity and prestige over the years, and is currently an official event in the International Federation of Competitive

Eating. In 1972, the first year the competition was on the books, winner Jason Schecter ate fourteen hot dogs and buns. Compare that to the 61 hot dogs and buns Joey Chestnut downed in ten minutes to win the 2014 crown.

Competitive eating got America's attention when Takeru Kobayashi came on the scene in 2001. This skinny Japanese man ate fifty hot dogs and buns in 2001, *doubling* the previous record. Kobayashi brought a special method to the table: he broke each hot dog in half, dipped each bun in water, and stuffed this medley all in his mouth at once. The soggy concoction slid down his throat with relative ease. He named his approach "The Solomon Method" after a Bible passage in which Solomon tests two women's love for a child by instructing them to cut the child in half. Luckily, the stakes are much lower when breaking a hot dog in half.

Because he looked nothing like the typical image Americans pictured at eating contests—essentially, a big, fat dude—Americans started paying extra attention to what was now considered a sport. Kobayashi dominated for six years before San Jose native and human vacuum cleaner Joey Chestnut out-ate him for the mustard yellow belt in 2007. That year, Chestnut finished 66 hot dogs and buns, three more than Kobayashi. The following year, Chestnut and Kobayashi were tied with 59 hot dogs after ten minutes. The contest went into overtime. Officials placed five hot dogs before each competitor. Whoever finished all five dogs and buns first would be declared the winner. In just fifty seconds, Chestnut cleaned his plate for the win. Chestnut beat Kobayashi the following year again, but Kobayashi stopped participating in 2010. Chestnut won his eighth consecutive title in 2014. But in 2015, his reign came to an end when Matthew Stonie ate 62 hot dogs and Chestnut stomached just 60.

Whether or not you're a fan of competitive eating or hot dogs themselves, the rags to riches story behind Nathan's is one of true grit and hustle, ingredients that are far more important than what goes into a hot dog.

PETER LUGER STEAK HOUSE

178 BROADWAY, BROOKLYN, NY 11211

(718) 387-7400 | WWW.PETERLUGER.COM

I knew I was getting close to Peter Luger when I smelled the meat. Still two blocks away, the unmistakable scent of beef wafted through my nostrils.

In 1887, German immigrant Carl Luger opened Carl Luger's Café Billiards and Bowling Alley in Williamsburg, Brooklyn. His son Peter wanted to follow in his father's footsteps, but with his own flair. When Carl passed away, Peter rebranded his father's business as a steak house. He renamed the place after himself, and the Peter Luger Steak House became a renowned beef destination that thrives today.

When Peter Luger passed away in 1941, his son Frederick took over the steakhouse. But he lacked his father's and grandfather's business savvy. For instance, Frederick was rumored to not even weigh deliveries. Plus, the changing community had not been good for business. A sizable Hasidic population had moved in to the neighborhood, and their religion prohibited them from eating the beef that Peter Luger served. And so by 1950, Peter Luger Steak House was on the auction block.

Sol Forman ran a metal-ware business across the street. For a quarter of a century, he had been known to eat one or two steaks a day at Peter Luger's. So when the restaurant went on the market, a faithful customer became its new owner. "Not knowing anything about the restaurant [industry] they just kind of went for it," says Sol's great-grandson David Berson, Peter Luger's current general manager of operations. Sol and his wife, Marsha, dove head first into the business, making high-quality beef their number one priority.

Marsha took charge of meat selection. For two years, she studied the trade with retired meat inspector Joe Dowd. Bi-weekly, she threw on a white coat (and a fur hat) to inspect and select USDA Prime beef. When a piece of meat met her approval, Marsha stamped it with a customized Peter Luger stamp. She passed the trade down to her daughters Marilynn and Amy, who passed it down to David, her grandson.

"I went to the meat market when I was probably fourteen years old," says Berson. "It's sensory overload. You're in this cold room, and there are odd body parts from cows everywhere . . . I was worried I'd be a vegetarian." Thankfully, he adapted. "I don't think there's any vegetarians in our family. It would be a kind of taboo subject."

Along with three other family members, Berson makes weekly trips to hand-select meat at various meat markets. "We start from a high quality perspective," Berson says, focused only on certified prime beef, which accounts for only about 2 to 3 percent of all beef in the United States. After marking the meat with personalized stamps, it's set aside and sent to the restaurant for dry aging. The dry-aging process reduces the collagen within meat. Collagen gives the meat a tough texture. Dry aging makes the beef more tender. Peter Luger's Brooklyn location—there is a second in Great Neck, Long Island—has three dry-age rooms. Meat spends an average of one month in the dry-age locker. At any given time, Peter Luger has "legitimately tons and tons" of meat on its premises, according to Berson.

The food at Peter Luger has remained consistent. You know what to expect. "We're not gonna serve you some kind of esoteric beef that's some kind of special," assures Berson. At lunchtime, Peter Luger offers burgers. But they're not available at dinner, when the restaurant dishes out its most popular items like filet mignon, sirloin steak, and a porterhouse.

The restaurant also added seafood to the menu in the 1980s. Reportedly, the restaurant made this addition to appease wives who accompanied their husbands but didn't want to eat red meat. This feminist thinks

that plenty of men enjoy fish and that the 1980s saw a growing number of vegetarians. Regardless, you come to Peter Luger Steak House for steak. But for the man or woman who's here to socialize instead of embrace their inner carnivore, other options are available, like the humongous slices of

tomato and onions that pair perfectly with the table steak sauce or the baked potato and creamed spinach.

Peter Luger's neighborhood and clientele have evolved over the years. Most noticeably, Williamsburg has become a trendy area beloved by hipsters. When Berson ate at Peter Luger as a kid, part of the restaurant's appeal was that it was an adventure outside of Manhattan. Venturing into Williamsburg has lost its novelty because it has become so gentrified. The restaurant's lunch business has enjoyed an influx of Korean, Japanese, and Chinese tourists.

For a long time, Peter Luger resisted joining the modern world of credit cards. The once cash and debit-card-only restaurant now accepts just one credit card: the Peter Luger credit card. As of 2001, 80,000 Peter Luger credit cards had been issued. Now, that number totals about 90,000. Still, for those paying by cash, waiters calculate the bills by hand and process payment with a manual cash register.

"I don't think we're doing anything magic," reflects Berson. "As Sol would say, [it's] 'simple goodness.'"

QUEENS & LONG ISLAND

THE BEER GARDEN AT BOHEMIAN HALL

29-19 24TH AVENUE ASTORIA, QUEENS, NY 11102

(718) 274-4925 | BOHEMIANHALL.COM

For a little piece of Czech and Slovakian culture, you don't have to head to Central Europe. Instead, take the N or Q train to Astoria Boulevard and order a beer and schnitzel at The Beer Garden at Bohemian Hall.

Astoria has been a stronghold of Bohemian culture since the mid-nineteenth century. While today "Bohemian" may likely conjure images of Mary-Kate Olsen in an oversized dress, Bohemia was once a kingdom that belonged to the Holy Roman Empire and then the Austrian Empire. Its territory comprised a section of Czechoslovakia and, today, is a large section of the Czech Republic. Bohemian can refer to both Czechs and Slovaks.

During the reign of the Austro-Hungarian Empire, many Czech and Slovak immigrants came to the United States and settled on the east side of Manhattan or in Astoria, Queens. In 1892, some of these immigrants formed the Bohemian Citizens' Benevolent Society of Astoria to maintain and celebrate Czech and Slovak culture.

In 1910, the society built a structure to serve as their base of operations. Nine years later, they purchased farmland upon which they built a beer garden, the same year that Prohibition began. "It was the "perfect time to start a beer garden," jokes the garden's general manager Andrew Walters. Because the beer garden operated under the charter of a non-profit cultural center and was owned instead of rented, and because they employed certain "creative devices," Walters says the business was able to survive despite the temperance movement. Today, the business thrives as an incorporated for-profit beer garden that celebrates Czech and Slovakian culture.

The Czech Republic and Slovakia have had a difficult and at times contentious history. Currently two independent countries, they have been

both unified and separate states. Both countries were part of the Austro-Hungarian Empire. When the empire collapsed after World War I in 1918, Czechs and Slovaks created a joint country called Czechoslovakia. Between World War I and World War II, tension grew between Czechs and Slovaks. The Slovaks broke off and formed Slovakia at the start of World War II. They allied with Nazi Germany. The Nazis occupied what was left of the former Czechoslovakia. After the war, the Czechs and Slovaks reunited once again to re-form Czechoslovakia. But they fell under the communist control of the Soviet Union until 1989, during which the "Velvet Revolution" replaced communism with democracy. The Czechs and Slovaks participated in a peaceful "Velvet Divorce" in 1993 to form two separate democratic states called the Czech Republic and Slovakia. Both countries are members of the European Union. All of these events and conflicts inspired Czech and Slovak immigration to New York.

General Manager Andrew Walters argues that stepping into The Beer Garden at Bohemian Hall is truly like experiencing a European beer garden. European beer gardens are "transforming," says Walter. "Pop culture has had a direct effect on them. I really feel you have a greater feeling of a European beer garden in Astoria, New York, than in Europe." The Beer Garden at Bohemian Hall sticks to its roots by holding traditional Czech and Slovakian festivals and serving beers and food that celebrates these cultures.

The establishment's head and sous chefs both hail from Slovakia. Their recipes have "truly [been] passed down hundreds and hundreds of years," says Walters. The recipes include traditional Czech dishes like *Tlacenka*, *Utopenec*, and potato pancakes. Other traditional items include a Baked *Palacinka* [crepes], potato pierogies, beef goulash, schnitzel, and apple strudel.

As far as beer goes, "You'll never see Budweiser on draft," promises Walters. The Beer Garden "keep[s] it European." The most popular beer on draft is Pilsner Urquell, a lager that has been brewed in Plzen, Czech Republic, since 1842. Other European beers on draft include BrouCzech, Hofbrau Summer Ale, and Schofferhofer. By drinking authentic Czech and Slovakian beers, you are not only experiencing Czechoslovakian culture, but paying for its continuation: "The sale of beer pays for the school," Walters points out. Indeed, beer garden sales fund the Bohemian Citizens' Society educational programs for children and adults.

The beer garden is truly a hidden gem. From the street, high walls conceal the garden. It's very easy to walk past not knowing what waits inside if the gates are closed. And when you're inside, it's easy to tune the rest of the world out. The space is large and accommodates about 5,000 people on an average weekend in the spring and summer. Rows of picnic tables under trees provide plenty of seating, and ample open space can accommodate cultural performances or patrons in the mood to dance.

The beer garden is open year-round. So if you've got a hankering for strudel and Hoegaarden, don't let the cold weather stop you. Head inside to the basement restaurant, a small space with red and white-checkered tablecloths that offers a break from the elements.

The National Register of Historic Places recognized Bohemian Hall as a Traditional Cultural Property (TCP) in 2000. The Register gives the TCP classification to places that currently promote cultural and community heritage. Unlike other places on the register, whose significance and impact relate to the past, a TCP location has an ongoing impact. To be a part of that impact, head to the Hall.

NEIR'S TAVERN

87-48 78TH ST, WOODHAVEN, NY 11421

(718) 296-0600 | NEIRSTAVERN.COM

Long before Kentucky's Churchill Downs or New Jersey's Meadowlands, horses raced for glory at Woodhaven, New York's Union Course track. When New York repealed its nineteen-year ban on horseracing in 1821—instituted because the sport incited rioting, public intoxication, and lewd behavior—thousands flocked to Woodhaven to watch horses race the four-mile loop.

During the early nineteenth century, southern horses typically outpaced northern horses. "Match races" pitted northern horses against southern horses in regional competitions that took on added significance as tensions grew before the American Civil War. Eight years after the Union

Course opened, a tavern popped up across the street. Known then as The Old Abbey, it met the libation needs of horseracing fans in the 1830s and continues to serve the community today.

On May 23, 1823, all eyes were on the Union Course, 60,000 pairs of eyes to be exact. Thousands were on hand to watch northern horse Eclipse take on southern stallion Sir Henry. Congress took the day off. The stock exchange closed. Presidential candidate Andrew Jackson even took a break from campaigning to attend. People bet their houses and slaves on the race.

By all measures, Eclipse was the underdog. Older and heavier, he was not the favorite. In those days, horses raced in "best of three" heats. Sir Henry won the first heat, setting a new American record for four miles in 7:37. Eclipse rallied to edge out Sir Henry in the second heat, sending the horses into a tie-breaking third heat. Eclipse won the third heat by three horse lengths, a symbolic victory for the North in an increasingly divisive country.

As tensions between North and South escalated to the point of war, the Union Course shut down, and Neir's Tavern grew more and more rowdy. According to current owner Loycent Gordon, Neir's "became known as a place for thieves" and the "unscrupulous type." In 1898, Louis Neir bought the bar and renamed it after himself. He added a bowling alley and ballroom to the tavern, attracting performers such as Mae West. Neir turned the tavern into a neighborhood hangout. The bar stayed in the Neir family until 1967, when another family took over until 2009.

As time passed and regulars aged, Neir's fell out of favor in the community. But Gordon is trying to reestablish Neir's as an important watering hole for locals. He's not focused on attracting clientele from all over or on competing with trendy Manhattan bars. The reality is: Neir's is out of the way for anybody but locals. From Manhattan, it's at least an hour's trip by subway. So now and then, for Manhattanites looking for a good neighborhood bar and a great burger, Neir's may be your destination. But as far as dependable business goes, Neir's relies on its own community to keep doors open.

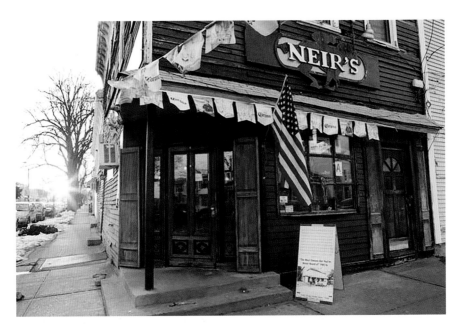

Neir's is a working class bar without frills or airs. Gordon and his bartenders greet patrons when they enter. Green-and-white-checkered tablecloths match the green walls. Wooden chairs and wooden floors feel as weathered as the bar's history. A huge TV is tuned to sports matches. The walls feature photographs of Neir's over the years—the oldest one dating back to 1898—as well as stills from movies shot in the bar and a collage of photos of some of the regulars.

One bookcase features a set of encyclopedias. The story goes that in the days before Siri had all the answers, a regular at Neir's always got into fights. He'd come home worked up and consult his encyclopedias to see if he'd been right or wrong. Fed up, his wife brought his collection of encyclopedias to the bar so that he'd be able to settle his arguments on the spot.

In the late 1980s, Martin Scorsese filmed *Goodfellas* at Neir's Tavern. When Queens-born firefighter Gordon took over, he sought to make Neir's a spot that welcomes artists both established and emerging. So he's opened the tavern to big budget films like *Tower Heist* and student filmmakers alike. "I open up the place to poets [and] directors that want to showcase their films," says Gordon. He also fashioned a very small stage where local comedians and singers can develop their talents. These events are always linked to the community. "Next month, comedy night is a kickoff for a food drive," Gordon tells me on a fall night.

Patrons of Neir's can count on a good beer and burger. Actually, a great burger. The Goodfellas burger is doused with a spicy sauce that should be bottled and sold. Fries are big, soft, and especially salty. Beers are classic with offerings like Budweiser and Guinness. In his effort to involve the local community, Gordon also features an IPA from a brewer making beer just a few blocks away.

As both a firefighter and tavern keeper, Gordon's trying to preserve and protect his community. He and the bartenders make an effort to know their customers by name and give a welcome tour of the space to new guests. In the past, it was in style for a regular at Neir's to buy a new customer's first beer. Gordon has seen that trend revive recently. His efforts to restore Neir's as a welcoming community spot seems to be working. "I'm not here for a bag of money," he says. "I really care." Rather than making a concerted effort to keep Neir's in his family, Gordon aims to make Neir's a sustainable business that serves the community long after he's gone.

Once a spot where racial and regional tensions played out with horses and booze, Neir's is now a bar whose staff and clientele reflect the diversity that defines New York City. For a welcoming environment, a cold beer, and a great burger, jockey over to Neir's.

TWEED'S RESTAURANT AND BUFFALO BAR

17 E MAIN ST, RIVERHEAD, NY 11901

(631) 237-8120 | WWW.TWEEDSRESTAURANTRIVERHEAD.COM

Before Springsteen, there was another Boss in town. His birth certificate said William Magear Tweed, but everybody called him "Boss" Tweed. Tweed ran the Democratic Party's political machine Tammany Hall during the 1860s and 70s. Along with his "Tweed Ring" of cronies, Boss Tweed controlled New York's elections, city appointments, and the Treasury. His big public works projects lined his own pockets.

For a long time, Boss was untouchable and even beloved. He did create a lot of public works, and his out-for-yourself attitude resonated with many New Yorkers. In particular, Irish immigrants, plagued by the "Irish Need Not Apply" days of discrimination, supported Tweed.

But the last straw came in 1871, when Tweed's New York County Courthouse project exceeded its 1858 budget of $250,000 many times over, racking up $12 million in costs by the time the building was completed in 1871. Known as "Tweed Court," much of the courthouse's budget ended up in Tweed's bank account. And he wasn't shy about showcasing it. On occasion, he traveled by private yacht and private railway car. From 1869 to 1871 alone, New York's debt climbed from $36.3 million to $97 million. Money talks, and it was fed up with Tweed.

Political cartoons by Thomas Nast famously criticized Tweed and recruited opponents. And in 1871, when a disgruntled former associate gave *The New York Times* a paper trail that incriminated Tweed, it was game over. Tweed served two years for forgery and larceny, but, in a feat fit for his stature, escaped from prison. He hid in Spain before Spanish officials flushed him out and returned him to the United States. He died in prison in 1878.

Eighteen years later, a restaurant opened in the J.J. Sullivan Hotel in Riverhead, Long Island, named in honor of the original Boss: Tweed's

Restaurant. Suffolk County's seat was located in Riverhead, so Boss Tweed had personally frequented the J.J. Sullivan Hotel along with future Tammany leader Charles Murphy.

During Prohibition, the restaurant didn't miss a beat: They put a barber chair out front and offered haircuts. But behind the salon, alcohol beckoned. And with Tammany Hall calling the shots, Prohibition was more of a joke than a law here. The Boss would have approved.

The Sullivan family owned the hotel and restaurant until local businessman and farmer Ed Tuccio took over. Long before Tweed and Tammany Hall, Ed Tuccio's family arrived on Long Island. They settled in North Folk in 1639. Tuccio brought his love for bison to Tweed's, turning it into Tweed's Restaurant and Buffalo Bar.

Tuccio has about 300 bison on his 500-acre bison farm and he's sold "thousands and thousands" of bison burgers at Tweed's in the last four decades. Tweed's bison menu also includes a bison T-bone, cowboy steak, filet mignon, hanger steak, and 5 pounds of bison chop meat.

Bison has risen in popularity since it was first sold commercially in the United States in the 1960s. Its popularity surged in the 80s, and after a period of decline from 1999–2003, it bounced back. As of the 2012 Census

of Agriculture, there were 187,000 bison in the United States, and bison producers operated in every state.

That's pretty impressive, considering bison came close to extinction at the end of the nineteenth century. Bison provided not only meat, but their wool was used for clothing, their fat used for soap, and hooves used for glue. An absence of laws protecting bison led to their significant depopulation. About 40 million bison roamed the US in 1800. That number dwindled to less than 1,000 by 1900. The Bronx Zoo basically saved bison from extinction when they preserved a herd in the early twentieth century. Most of today's bison can be traced back to this group.

If you're like me before this book came out, you weren't really sure what the difference is between buffalo and bison. The words are used interchangeably in the American lexicon, and while both belong to the cattle family, there are some differences. The most obvious is their horns: buffalo have bigger horns than bison. Bison also have a shoulder hump, while buffalo do not.

Even simpler? No buffalo have ever lived in North America. They're all bison. When explorers landed in the New World, they thought that bison

looked like Old World buffalo. The name stuck. Just like Columbus called Native Americans Indians, we have a history of misnaming things and not correcting ourselves.

Bison meat is a healthy alternative to cow. It is very lean. Low in cholesterol, fat, and calories, it's high in protein. After looking down at the bison on your plate at Tweed's, look up at the bison head on the wall. Reportedly, it's the last bison Teddy Roosevelt ever shot in 1883. It ended up in Tuccio's hands by chance. "A friend of mine called me. He ran the town dump," recalls Tuccio. Tuccio's friend spotted the bison head in the trash, discarded by a group of Boy Scouts. He asked Tuccio if he'd like it. Tuccio responded with an enthusiastic, "Sure I want it." The head of this bison shot in the Dakota Territories tells the story of regulation-free hunting: "He went out to the Dakotas on that famous hunt," says Tuccio. "[He] was absolutely shocked that there were no animals left. Not only had they shot all the buffalo . . . there were no deer, there were no anything."

While most people come to Tweed's for the bison, Tuccio also specializes in seafood. His high standards define the kitchen. "I'm a commercial clammer myself," he says. "I grew up on the bay. For me, there is no compromise when it comes to shellfish. It's got to be the best."

Tuccio champions Long Island's agricultural prowess. "Long Island is a poster child for agri-tourism," says Tuccio. The island offers wineries, microbreweries, farms, and Tuccio's own bison farm, the largest one east of the Mississippi. Unlike other parts of the country, where farms border farms for miles, Long Island's farms are very close to dense urban populations. "We don't have to go looking for the market," explains Tuccio. "The market comes to us."

The atmosphere at Tweed's provides links to the past. The mahogany and marble bar was featured at the 1893 World Exposition in Chicago. The restaurant features its original Victorian chandeliers, stained class, fireplace, and ceiling. So for a bisoned bite of history, head to Tweed's in Riverhead.

THE BRONX

YANKEE TAVERN

72 E 161ST ST, BRONX, NY 10451

(718) 292-6130 | WWW.YANKEETAVERN.NYC

Full disclosure: I'm a Mets fan. But even I can admit that the Yankees are New York's pride and joy. From Babe Ruth to Derek Jeter, the Yankees have dazzled and united New Yorkers for over a century. With twenty-seven World Series Championships under their belt as of 2009, they have far more rings than any other team in Major League Baseball. And ever since the Yankees began playing at Yankee Stadium, their fans and players have been clinking glasses at Yankee Tavern.

Baseball developed as an offshoot of cricket and rounders, a game played by colonists in New England. The New York Knickerbocker Baseball Club formed in 1845 and one of its members, Alexander Joy Cartwright, developed a set of rules that basically established baseball as we know it. Those rules included three strikes and you're out, the establishment of foul lines, and a diamond infield. Cartwright also did away with a previous practice of throwing the ball directly at a runner's body to get him out. The sport grew in popularity.

The National League of Professional Baseball Clubs formed in 1876. The American League followed in 1901. The leagues competed for the first World Series in 1903.

The Yankee franchise originated in Baltimore in 1901 as part of the American League. Two years later, Frank Farrell and Bill Devery purchased the franchise and relocated it to New York City. They played at Hilltop Park in Washington Heights, Manhattan, from 1903 to 1912 as the New York Highlanders. Writers referred to the players as Yankees, perhaps because they played so far uptown that borrowing a northern nickname from the American Civil War seemed appropriate. The team relocated to the Polo Grounds

in Manhattan in 1913, and management officially renamed the team The New York Yankees.

Construction began on a new stadium for the Yankees in 1922. After 284 days of labor, the team played its first game at Yankee Stadium in the Bronx on April 18, 1923, against the Boston Red Sox. The Yankees won 4 to 1 before a crowd of 74,200.

Journalists and fans nicknamed the team the Bronx Bombers and the Pinstripers for their striped uniforms. They called the stadium "The House That Ruth Built" for Babe Ruth, the star slugger the Yankees acquired from the Red Sox in 1920. With Ruth, the franchise won its first World Championship in 1923.

That same year, the Yankee Tavern opened just outside Yankee Stadium on 161st street. The joint has catered to baseball fans and players ever since. Yankee Tavern bills itself as "the original sports bar." It's a spacious, grimy beer and wings kind of place. Photos and paintings of Yankee Stadium and Yankee players clutter the walls. The tavern has two separate areas: the bar and a seating area. The bar is very long and features five televisions. A KISS pinball machine and bowling arcade game feel at home, but an electronic jukebox feels out of place.

The dining area is split level, with three rows of mismatching tables and chairs and seven televisions. Two large murals, one of Yankee Stadium and another of players in uniform, add a nice change to the photos that take up most wall space. Many of the chairs and blue booth cushions are worse for the wear, and the wood floors have been badly scuffed up. A New York City Football Club decal is literally scotch taped to the wall.

But you didn't come here for a fine dining experience. You came here for beer, sports, and grub. On that, Yankee Tavern delivers. From wings and mozzarella sticks to burgers and personal pizzas, the casual menu befits the vibe. The menu features appetizers like chicken fingers and baked clams as well as a variety of pastas and salads. The kitchen also churns out sandwiches, wraps, tacos, burgers, and hot dogs. Pork chop and grilled chicken platters are also available with rice and beans.

Players who have patronized the tavern include Babe Ruth, Lou Gehrig, Mickey Mantle, and Billy Martin. In the offseason, cops and lawyers working at the nearby State Supreme Court and Criminal Court gather at the Tavern along with steelworkers and locals. On a Halloween afternoon after the Yankees' season has ended, a small gathering of men boisterously trade stories and laugh at the end of the bar while local kids come in to collect treats from the bar.

The Yankees moved into a new $1.3 billion stadium across the street in 2009. In their final game at the original Yankee Stadium Derek Jeter gave a speech to the crowd:

"We're relying on you to take the memories from this stadium and add them to the new memories that come to the new Yankee Stadium, and continue to pass them on from generation to generation. On behalf of this

entire organization, we want to take this moment to salute you, the greatest fans in the world."

The new Yankee Stadium has hundreds of food options. Gone are the days of keeping it simple with hot dogs and beer. Today's baseball fans can enjoy the game *and* honor their diets. In addition to greasy staples from franchises like Johnny Rockets, Papa Johns, and Nathan's Famous, patrons can keep it lighter with Farmers Market and a gluten-free New York Grill.

This may seem great to stadium goers, but it has posed problems for Yankee Tavern. The first day the new stadium opened, owner Joe Bastone's food sales plummeted by a whopping 75 percent. He lowered prices and food sales crept back up but never matched what the tavern made before the new stadium. But Yankee Tavern's still standing seven years later. With a history as long as the stadium it borders, it's a staple in Yankee and Bronx history.

STATEN ISLAND

KILLMEYER'S OLD BAVARIAN INN

4254 ARTHUR KILL ROAD, STATEN ISLAND, NY 10309

(718) 984-1202 | WWW.KILLMEYERS.COM

G ermans have had a significant presence on Staten Island since the mid-nineteenth century. About 200,000 Germans immigrated to New York City by 1860, and many settled on Staten Island. They imbued the island with German culture by setting up German-American organizations, festivals, and businesses. One German business that has survived since 1859 is Killmeyer's Old Bavarian Inn.

While some German immigrants flocked to Staten Island by choice, others ended up here by force. When ships sailed in to New York Harbor, a health inspector checked everyone before the ship even docked. If the inspector flagged anyone aboard as potentially contagious, he redirected the entire ship to Staten Island's Tomkinsville Quarantine Station. Thousands of Germans spent their first night on American soil inside this quarantine hospital. First class passengers enjoyed their stay in a more luxurious part of the complex known as St. Nicholas Hospital. Steerage passengers, however, slept in bunkhouses.

The residents of Tomkinsville opposed the quarantine station, especially after yellow fever epidemics spread beyond quarantine borders in 1848 and 1856. By 1858, locals had reached their breaking point. On September 1, thirty men turned to arson. Arsonists arranged for the sixty people in the hospital to be relocated before they set fire to the buildings. Fire departments arrived, but claimed that their hoses did not work. They happily watched the quarantine station burn. Police either ignored their calls or were chased away by pelted rocks. No one died. Operation leaders Richard Thompson and Ray Tomkins went on trial, but their lawyers argued that the quarantine station posed such a danger to public health that their clients

had acted out of self-defense. They won. A floating ship replaced the quarantine station. In 1866, the quarantine ship was docked near the landfill at South Beach, Staten Island, and eventually moved to Ellis Island.

Amidst this drama, Germans settled on Staten Island. By 1873, ten German American breweries operated in the borough. Over the next few decades, Germans solidified their presence on the island with German organizations, festivals, and businesses. Three German newspapers circulated on Staten Island: *Der Deutsche Staten Islander*, *Staten Island Deutsche Zeitung*, and the *Staten Island Post*. German philanthropists also left their mark on Staten Island by funding Tappen Park, the Staten Island University Hospital, and the Staten Island Academy.

Killmeyer's Old Bavarian Inn sits on property that belonged to Balthazar Kreischer, the owner of the Kreischer Brick Manufactory. His profound influence on the area led to it being called Kreischerville. German immigrant Nicholas Killmeyer purchased the property from Kreischer in 1859. He operated the property as a barbershop and saloon. His children added a hotel on the second floor in the late nineteenth century. In 1945, Reuben Simonson and his son Cappy purchased the property. It operated as a tavern for the next fifty years. In the 1970s and 1980s it became a hub for musicians including Twisted Sister ("We're Not Gonna Take It"). Current owner Ken Tirado describes it as "a hugely successful roadhouse" and a "notorious bucket of blood" in those years. When Tirado bought the space in 1995, he wanted the restaurant to return to its German roots. After World War I and World War II, the neighborhood had become less openly German. In response to anti-German sentiment, establishments that once celebrated their German roots and culture closed or rebranded. The neighborhood even changed its name from Kresicherville to Charleston in order to appear more Anglo-Saxon.

Although Tirado does not have any German blood, he wanted to fill a void for the German community and redesign the tavern as a German place once again. He had worked for years in the theater industry as a scenic designer and put that work experience to use in the restaurant's makeover.

He traveled to Munich to do his research. He visited breweries and beer gardens and fell in love with their aesthetic. "They're so cool" and "so visual" he says. He modeled his garden after those he observed in Germany. Rectangular stones pave the way toward a wooden gazebo and bar underneath a large structure that looks like half a barn. The beer garden operates from May through Halloween. During that time, thousands of patrons pour through his doors on an average weekend. "This is my season," he says. "I know I'm gonna be able to pay some bills."

Inside, the Happy Tones oom-pah band plays every Sunday. Beer barrels and crests hang from the ceiling and walls. A stained glass picture of the German castle, Neuschwanstein, hangs on the wall. Fun fact: This castle reportedly inspired Disney's Magic Kingdom.

The menu features classic German fare. Of course, that includes plenty of sausage and schnitzel, brisket, goulash, and *flammkuchen*, a traditional German pizza featuring bacon, onion, and crème fraîche. The kitchen also flips burgers and makes sandwiches.

Only two decades ago this neighborhood was much more rural. You can still ride horse trails nearby; hitching posts stood where cars now park. As part of his effort to clean up the city's vices, Mayor Rudy Giuliani designated certain areas off-limits to strip clubs. Sex-oriented establishments could not do business within 500 feet of homes, schools, churches, or each other as of 1995. A strip club called Curves, following the guidelines, popped up less than a mile north

of the inn. To keep his establishment on the up and up, Tirado likes to close by 1:00 a.m. As he explains, the only people coming to Killmeyer's that late are the people who got kicked out of Curves or another strip club.

Driving around Killmeyer's neighborhood, it's easy to see why Tirado calls this neighborhood "the last frontier on Staten Island." Construction machines are hard at work everywhere developing the area. The film and television industry has been expanding to Staten Island as of late. The TV show *Limitless* and the film *Little Children* both staged scenes at Killmeyer's, and Broadway Stages purchased the decommissioned Arthur Kill Correctional Facility from the state for $7 million in 2014. It will invest another $20 million to transform it into a 69-acre property featuring sound stages and studios.

When New Yorkers were priced out of Manhattan, they went to Brooklyn. When they were priced out of Brooklyn, they went to Queens. Next up, I predict the Bronx and Staten Island will have their moments as a real estate developer's canvas. Grab a beer and bratwurst at Killmeyer's and watch it happen.

A BRIEF HISTORY OF THE HUDSON VALLEY

The year was 1607. It was the Age of Exploration. European powers seeking new trade routes and economic opportunities sponsored sailors charting new courses across unknown waters. Fifteenth and sixteenth century explorers had opened the Americas to Europe, paving the way for major colonization efforts in the 1600s. That year, the Muscovy Company of London hired British explorer Henry Hudson to find a shorter trade route from Europe to Asia by sailing through the Arctic Ocean. Hudson hit a patch of ice in the Svalbard archipelago and could not finish. But the Muscovy Company hired him again the following year to make the journey between Svalbard and Novaya Zemlya. Again, he hit ice and had to return home. After two failed trips, British investors had lost their faith in Hudson. But the Dutch thought the third time would be the charm.

In 1609, the Dutch East India Company hired Hudson to find a Northwest Passage to the New World. He set sail from Holland aboard the *Half Moon* in 1609. He hit rough waters. His contract required him to turn back. But he pressed on. He went ashore in Newfoundland, Canada, and then sailed south. That part of the voyage took him to the river that would one day bear his name. On that trip up the river he sailed as far as present-day Albany.

On his next expedition from 1610 to 1611, funded by the British East India, the Muscovy Companies, and private investors, Hudson sailed on the *Discovery* and spent months in the Hudson Bay, believing it to be the Pacific Ocean. His disgruntled crew believed that Hudson had been unfairly distributing rations to his favorite crewmembers. So before making the trip back to England, these irritated crewmembers led a mutiny. They set Hudson, his son John, and seven crewmembers with scurvy adrift in a lifeboat in the Hudson Bay. They were never heard from again.

Hudson's travels led to the colonization of the area we now call the Hudson Valley, the area along both sides of the Hudson River above New York City and north to Albany. For the first half of the seventeenth century, the Hudson Valley operated mostly under Dutch control. Under Director General Peter Stuyvesant, the Dutch established present-day Kingston as a Stockade District in New Netherland, the Dutch colony in North America, to protect Dutch settlers.

In 1664, Great Britain ordered the Dutch to surrender and cede their American territories. They didn't put up a fight and New Netherland became New York.

During the American Revolution, both the Americans and the British wanted to control the Hudson River. The British reasoned that if they controlled the river, they would weaken American defenses by cutting the colonies in half. The British fought the Battle of Saratoga in an effort to gain control of the Hudson River, but the Continental Army won. This victory convinced the French to join the American cause. British and American forces fought several battles in the Hudson Valley, and Washington established his headquarters in numerous parts of the region throughout the war. The area has maintained an important role in military history since the establishment of the U.S. Military Academy at West Point in 1802.

Beginning in the 1920s, the Catskill Mountains region of the Hudson Valley became a haven for Jewish hotels and resorts, earning the nicknames the Borscht Belt, Solomon County, and the Jewish Alps. When Jewish families began moving out of New York City and settling in this area at the turn of the century, those families began to rent out rooms to wealthy city Jews who could afford to vacation. These small operations grew into huge ventures. Due to anti-Semitism, many Jews preferred to vacation at Jewish-owned facilities, and the Borscht Belt had hundreds to choose from. Grossinger's, for example, grew from a modest seven-room farmhouse to an

812-acre property with an Olympic-sized skating rink and swimming pool, tennis courts, three ski slopes with imported snow, a 1,500-seat nightclub, and its own landing strip.

Gigantic properties like Grossinger's, Kutscher's, and the Concord revolutionized hospitality with "all inclusive" packages that covered meals, sports, and entertainment. These resorts boasted huge venues where musicians and comedians performed. Jerry Seinfeld cut his teeth performing stand-up in the Borscht Belt, as did Rodney Dangerfield and Woody Allen.

Smaller hotels or bungalow colonies didn't have these ostentatious features, but their guests helped stimulate the region's economy by patronizing local restaurants, movie theaters, and shops.

But the Borscht Belt lost its luster by the 1960s. Historians blame the three As: air conditioning, airfare, and assimilation. With air conditioning increasingly available in most places, people didn't have to visit the Catskills' cooler mountains or resort pools to escape the summer heat. Cheaper airfare also meant that vacation planners could increase their destination radius. And unlike their parents, assimilated third and fourth generation Jews didn't crave the self-segregation that these resorts afforded. A decline in anti-Semitism was great for morality, but bad for business as Jews felt comfortable seeking non-Jewish vacation experiences. The 1987 film *Dirty Dancing* takes place at a fictional Catskills resort, and the resort owner laments the Borscht Belt's decline: "It all seems to be ending. You think kids want to come with their parents to take foxtrot lessons? Trips to Europe! That's what the kids want."

Resorts closed by the dozen until only a ghost town remained. An area that once boasted over 500 hotels and 50,000 bungalows suffered devastating economic losses. Sullivan County is hoping to make a comeback with the introduction of a casino in the near future, but the process has proven slow.

While the Hudson Valley became a tourist destination, it also became an important manufacturing sector when IBM established its base of operations here in the 1940s. The company originally manufactured aircraft cannons before transitioning to office supplies and eventually computers. The computer boom made IBM a household name and established the Hudson Valley as a technology hub. IBM created thousands of jobs and pumped talent into the region. Jobs in retail, restaurant, and other industries followed to support all the "Beemers" living in the region. For five decades, IBM played a significant role in the Hudson Valley economy. But in 1993, the company fired 2,700 people. It was a huge blow.

While the Hudson Valley suffered great economic losses in hospitality and technology, its status as a culinary hub began and remains thanks to the Culinary Institute of America's move from New Haven, Connecticut, to the Hudson Valley in 1972. Many of the graduates remain in the area, infusing the valley with top-notch chefs and restaurants, some of which you'll read about in the following pages.

From the state government in Albany and down the Hudson to towns just outside of New York City, the Hudson Valley offers nature, history, and culinary treasures for your exploration and respite.

THE HUDSON VALLEY

THE '76 HOUSE

110 MAIN STREET, TAPPAN, NY 10983

(845) 359-5476 | WWW.76HOUSE.COM

The Dutch government required American colonists to establish a public house to conduct meetings, receive mail, and host travelers in order to be recognized as a settlement. In other words: They had to build a bar. Dutch immigrants who settled in Tappan established a public house in 1668 on present day Main Street. It still stands and is known as The '76 House.

The Tappan tribe of Native Americans lived in this area before the Dutch settled. When the Netherlands ceded its American territories to Great Britain, British immigration raised Tappan's population in the 1690s considerably.

During the American Revolutionary War, the tavern played an important role as a prison for British spy Major John André. In 1779, the British

forces made André head of British secret intelligence. American traitor Benedict Arnold reported to André, who passed information up to British General Henry Clinton. In 1780, Benedict Arnold delivered information about the American fort at West Point to André. André put the secret documents in his boot. But, when three men stopped André in an attempt to steal from him, they took his boots, and out fell the plans for West Point. They'd caught a spy. The would-be thieves delivered André to the American authorities. They jailed him at The '76 House.

But André's stay at the tavern was relatively nice. "Major André was wined and dined while he was held here," says Robert Norden, the current owner of The '76 House. "He had three lady callers," Norden even mentions. While imprisoned at The '76 House, André drew with charcoal, wrote a play, and even ate his meals with Continental Army officer Benjamin Tallmadge.

This might sound odd to the modern reader, but at the time, there was a high level of respect between officers on opposing sides. Washington even wanted to set André free in exchange for Benedict Arnold, who'd escaped to England, but the exchange never materialized. The American and British armies also had an unspoken rule that they would imprison rather than execute each other's captured officers, but André did not luck out. The Continental Congress had clearly established hanging as the punishment for spies in 1776, stating any persons "who shall be found lurking as spies . . . shall suffer death." And so, at the age of 31, André was hanged in Tappan on October 2, 1780, just a half mile up a hill from the public house that served as his prison.

Some Americans sympathized with André. Many thought of him as a talented military man in the wrong place at the wrong time. Even George Washington said, "He was more unfortunate than criminal, an accomplished man and a gallant officer."

A 1783 print titled *The Unfortunate Death of Major André* and an 1822 song "The Ballad of Major André" illustrate American sympathy for the British spy. Here are the lyrics to the ballad:

Now Arnold to New York has gone,
A-fighting for his King,
And left poor Major André
On the gallows for to swing.
André was executed,
He looked both meek and mild,
His face was fair and handsome,
And pleasantly he smiled.
It moved each eye with pity,
And every heart there bled,
And everyone wished him released
And Arnold in his stead.
He was a man of honor!
In Britain he was born,
To die upon the gallows
Most highly he did scorn.
And now his life has reached its end
So young and blooming still—
In Tappan's quiet countryside
He sleeps upon the hill.

American sculptor Cyrus W. Field even created a monument on the site of André's death in 1879. The rectangular granite boulder bears three inscriptions, including Washington's quote about André. The main inscription describes the circumstances of André's execution, stating, "His death, though according to the stern code of war, moved even his enemies to pity, and both armies mourned the fate of one so young and brave." A third Latin inscription from the *Aeneid*, written by Virgil, translated reads: "These are the tears of things, and our mortality cuts to the heart."

Not everyone approves of the André monument. It has been blown up twice. After the first incident, Field added a plaque that said, "Come one,

come all: this rock shall fly from its firm base as soon as I." Basically, an eloquent version of "over my dead body." Built on his personal property, Field felt that installing the monument was well within his rights. He added a spiky iron fence around the monument, but someone still managed to get in and put dynamite under it again. The monument still exists today, somewhat out of place among the modern homes that surround it. After your meal at The '76 House, it's worth the short drive or walk to the bizarre monument. For the modern viewer, it's hard to imagine erecting a statue to honor the enemy.

During World War II, The '76 House saw a lot of action once more when the Army processed 1.3 million troops at Camp Shanks in Tappan. Today, The '76 House attracts a variety of customers, including the Daughters of the American Revolution on the second Saturday of every month, who recited the Pledge of Allegiance one Saturday afternoon while I enjoyed lunch in the tavern.

Norden espouses a great enthusiasm for history, but never wants to have servers dressed in period costume or "Yankee Doodle" playing over the airwaves. "We don't rely on our pedigree as the oldest [tavern]," says Norden. Rather, he's trying to do the "same thing a tavern did three hundred years ago." That includes not only serving food, but also providing entertainment and a place to conduct business. As was probably the case in the early days of this public house, Norden observes a real estate or corporate transaction at The '76 House "at least once a day." The tavern also features live music every night and, appropriately, a classic American menu. The kitchen features "a lot of comfort food items that harken back to what folks enjoyed two hundred and fifty years ago," says Norden.

That includes lamb, venison, duck, and veal. If you're feeling patriotic, you can eat an entire Thanksgiving meal condensed on a baguette, featuring turkey, cranberries, and stuffing. Burgers, sandwiches, and salads are served, while entrees like venison seasoned with lingonberry demi-glace and mushroom ragout reach higher, as do the alligator empanadas and wild boar sausage appetizers. Eat off metal chargers made from imitation pewter. Unlike real pewter, they're made "without lead, so we don't kill our customers," Norden jokingly promises.

Order a craft beer or cocktail from the bar, above which guns from the American Revolutionary War, the American Civil War, and the Spanish-American War hang. If you dine at The '76 House, you'll join a long list of distinguished patrons, from George Washington and Alexander Hamilton to Robert DeNiro and Julia Roberts. So tie up your horse on the hitching posts outside the restaurant, or park your car in the lot, and eat in the Hudson Valley's most delicious prison.

Gray gold changed the world. Gold's more pragmatic cousin, "gray gold," also known as cement, revolutionized architecture and industry. And the discovery of gray gold in Rosendale, New York, defined the town in the nineteenth century. The 1850 House has been in operation since 1850, when gray gold made Rosendale a boomtown.

Engineer Canvass White stands at the center of the gray gold story. White began work on the Erie Canal in 1817. His boss, Benjamin Wright (aka the "Father of American Civil Engineering"), sent him to England in 1817 to study British engineering methods, which outpaced American efforts at the time. He returned with tools and information. In particular, he brought back an understanding of hydraulic cement necessary for building underground and constructing canal locks. England used stone and concrete for their canals. Too expensive to import, White knew he needed to find an American supply of concrete. He did so in Chittenango, New York. The Erie Canal used 500,000 bushels of White's product but never paid him for it.

Then in 1825, White hit the jackpot: He found a thirty-two-square-mile limestone deposit that stretched from High Falls north about ten miles to Kingston. The region became known as Rosendale. Present-day Rosendale sits between the two towns.

Heating limestone and adding water (aka "slaking") yields concrete. The cement became known as "Rosendale Cement" and went on to transform an industry and community.

Canvass and his brother Hugh created a cement company with plants in Rosendale; Louisville, Kentucky; and Cumberland, Maryland. Right away, engineers used Rosendale cement to build the locks in the Delaware &

Hudson Canal. The Brooklyn Bridge, fortified by Rosendale Cement, opened in 1883. The Statue of Liberty was finished in 1886, and its 27,000-ton pedestal was made from Rosendale cement. At its peak around 1898, Rosendale produced 3.5 million barrels of cement a year and operated fifteen plants. During that time, Rosendale contained 38 percent of the nation's cement plants and produced over 40 percent the country's total cement.

The town of Rosendale formed as a direct result of the cement industry. The area officially belonged to several towns but in an effort to put all the mining activity under one political umbrella, officials created the town of Rosendale in 1844.

MAIN STREET, SHOWING BAXTER'S STORE.   ROSENDALE, N.Y.

MAIN STREET, ROSENDALE, N.Y.

Rosendale thrived in the second half of the nineteenth century. Cement mining created thousands of jobs, including retail and hospitality that sprang up to support miners. The 1850 House was one example. Made from Rosendale Cement, the property opened around 1850 as the Central Hotel. Its name changed throughout the nineteenth and twentieth centuries. Most recently, it operated as the Astoria Hotel from the 1940s until 2011. Current proprietor and local resident Mike Ruger bought the hotel in 2001. He refurbished the property as an inn and renamed it for its history. The hotel opened as The 1850 House in 2012.

The space feels new and clean. Floorboards don't creak, and corners aren't cluttered with the grandmotherly charm that some bed and breakfasts favor. "I've been to a lot of B and B's," says Ruger, who has observed "all the tchotchkes." But "we don't do doileys here," he says. Instead, Ruger and business partner Kristen Tully have embraced modern decor while honoring the town's past with historical prints of Rosendale scattered throughout the first floor lobby, tavern, and in each of the inn's ten guest rooms. These prints show visitors what Rosendale's main street and cement caves looked like in years past.

The small tavern offers visitors a place to relax with a glass of wine or a bite to eat. The bar features local whiskies and micro-brews. The kitchen produces small plates like macaroni and cheese or chips and salsa alongside salads, flatbread pizza, and burgers. It opens at 4:00 p.m. every day except Monday and Tuesday and closes "when the last guest goes upstairs," says Ruger.

The 1850 House offers a number of separate spaces to enjoy, including the lobby, tavern, and even a small reading nook for two. Outside, The 1850 House has a lovely deck overlooking the Rondout Creek. Located on Rosendale's very small main street, The 1850 House is steps from several cafes and shops and a small movie theater all on Main Street. The colorful, quaint strip also boasts a Tibetan craft store, a cheese shop, a pickle store, and a tattoo parlor.

In recent years, the town has received an influx of city artists tired of paying high rents for minimal space who've made Rosendale home. The town has an artistic vibe in a natural setting that also attracts city dwellers for weekend get-

aways. Ruger says that these city escapees rent rooms at The 1850 House alongside patrons from Europe or locals living in a five-hour radius.

In 1825, Canvass White put Rosendale on the map with his discovery of gray gold. For a look at old meets new, stop by The 1850 House.

CROMWELL MANOR HISTORIC INN

174 ANGOLA ROAD, CORNWALL, NY 12518

(845) 534-7136 | WWW.CROMWELLMANORINN.COM

Like other Quaker families searching for religious freedom, the Cromwell family of England journeyed across the Atlantic to settle in colonial America. Led by patriarch David Cromwell, a descendant of Oliver Cromwell, they settled on a farm in Cornwall, New York. Today, the Cromwell Manor Historic Inn operates on that property.

The oldest structure on the 240-acre Cromwell family farm dates back to 1764. David and his wife, Rebecca, lived in the small house, which can be seen on the right when you enter the property. The large manor house he built, the first house of its size in the area, is the dominant building on the property. David and Rebecca had ten children, including their son James, a soldier in the Union Army. Despite his Quaker faith, which favors pacifism over war, James believed so strongly in the Union Army's cause that he enlisted in the Orange County regiment. He died at the age of 23 in the Battle of Gettsyburg (July 1–3, 1863).

The Cromwell family sold off some of their farmland in 1914 but remained in the home through 1957. That year, the Association of Retired Teachers purchased the property to use for summer retreats. The property became

the bed and breakfast that continues to operate today. Three owners have operated the business, and today Eileen Hartmann captains the operation.

"I grew up just across the road from it," says Hartmann. "I fell in love with it." She scooped up the property when it went on the market in 2012. The place had fallen into disrepair. "It became my personal mission to go in and rescue it," she says. "I like old things. I like restoring things." She has spent the last four years "bringing it back to grandeur." She has added a couple goats and begun farming on the property. "I don't think we own property," she argues. "I think we get entrusted with it."

Hartmann has observed three main groups of guests that visit the Cromwell Manor Historic Inn. The first consists of people affiliated with nearby West Point, be it tourists, graduates, or parents of students. Some stay at the inn and visit the nearby Purple Heart Museum, where the stories of 1.7 million Purple Heart recipients have been preserved. The second group is made up of affluent travelers interested in the Hudson Valley arts scene, in particular the Storm King Art Center. This 500-acre sculpture garden features sculptures, some massive and others small, from gigantic pieces in wide-open fields to smaller wonders visitors happen upon, positioned between trees on winding paths. You'll generate endorphins while you walk around the massive estate and feed your senses with striking works of art. And the last group that Hartmann

has noticed is New Yorkers looking to get out of the city for a weekend. They take advantage of local wineries and nature.

The Cromwell Manor Historic Inn features nine antique-filled guest rooms in the manor house and four in the 1764 house, whose basement operated as a tavern in its early days. The Manor features a pair of suites that often attract brides and bridesmaids.

Visitors eat breakfast at 8:30 or 10:30 a.m. in the dining room. Guests can count on an egg, starch, fruit, and protein to jumpstart their metabolisms. Items like poached pear compote, quiche, zucchini muffins, and fruit and granola parfaits have graced the inn's tables. The dining room features an impressive teapot collection.

The property no longer stretches for 240 acres, but now consists of seven acres for guests to wander. Sit on the backyard patio under a blue umbrella or rock in a white rocking chair on the front porch and admire the foreground's greenery and the mountains in the distance.

The property has a welcoming, tranquil vibe. From the dog named Brew who lives on the premises to the friendly staff, the bed and breakfast offers a pleasant escape from the city and proximity to many local attractions.

Hartmann says that to continue, the Cromwell Manor Historic Inn must add on to its offerings. "I'm not sure it can exist by itself as a B and B with the current economic climate," she worries. That's why she's added farming to the business, and the future might even include expanding breakfast service into a full-blown restaurant.

A family cemetery once existed on the property, but has since been dug up and the Cromwell bodies relocated. Still, Hartmann thinks there's a little bit of the Cromwell family that must still exist on the land. She hopes that "if they could look down they'd be happy with how we're treating the house now." Hartmann admits that she takes it very personally if guests don't love the house "because I love it so much." It might be hard to match the owner's enthusiasm, but head up the river to Cornwall and give it a try.

HOFFMAN HOUSE

94 N. FRONT STREET, KINGSTON, NY 12401

(845) 338 -2626 | WWW.HOFFMANHOUSETAVERN.COM

One of the first Dutch settlements, Kingston was home to New York's first state legislature. The town also had a stockade, making it an important site during colonists' battles with Native Americans and during the American Revolution. The Hoffman House, a home built in the seventeenth century within the Stockade District, remains intact and operates as a restaurant.

Ginny and Pat Bradley bought the Hoffman house in 1975. They renovated the dilapidated property and opened for business two years later. Dutch colonists used the Hoffman House as a lookout for members of the Esopus tribe of Lenape Native Americans during the Esopus Wars. "There are steps going up to the attic which went to the roof," says Ginny. "[The Dutch] would see [Native Americans] coming up and go down and warn settlers about [an] impending attack."

Kingston was originally named Esopus after the local tribe of Native Americans. When the Dutch settled the area in 1658, both sides were wary of one another but entered into trade anyway. Unfortunately, the Esopus contracted diseases and started drinking the colonists' alcohol. Both wreaked havoc on the native population. One night, a group of Dutchmen interpreted a raucous group of Esopus as antagonistic. In reality, they were just drinking, but the Dutch launched an attack on their neighbors. The Esopus responded by attacking Kingston and destroying crops and killing livestock. The opponents struck a truce in July 1660.

A second Esopus War broke out three years later. The Esopus tribe entered Kingston under the guise of trade but initiated a massacre instead.

They killed twelve men, four women, and two children inside the stockade. They kidnapped ten women and children and burned twelve homes.

The Dutch and Esopus signed a peace treaty the following year. Some historians argue that conflicts with Native Americans exhausted and weakened the Dutch so much that they basically surrendered New Netherland to Great Britain without firing a single shot on September 8, 1664. The British renamed the area New York after the Duke of York.

In 1707, Nicholas Hoffman bought the house, which would remain in his family for two centuries. The most famous member of his family was Anthony Hoffman, who served in the Provincial Congress of New York City in 1774 and signed the 1777 Articles of Confederation, the pre-cursor to the U.S. Constitution.

That year, Hoffman's hometown of Kingston went up in flames at the hands of the British. The British hoped to weaken the American colonies by seizing control of the Hudson River, to ostensibly cut the colonies in half by taking this strategic river. When the British seized New York City in 1776, the Patriots moved up the Hudson until they found Kingston—on a hill two miles from the river—to be the most secure place to set up camp. As the center of American operations, it was also a target. And on June 16, 1777, the British descended upon the town and burned it to the ground. Under the leadership of General John Vaughan, British soldiers turned 254 buildings into ash, including a church and the courthouse. In a report to his superiors, Vaughan wrote: *"On our entering the Town they fired from their Houses, which induced me to reduce the Place to Ashes, which I accordingly did, not leaving a house. We found a considerable Quantity of Stores of all kinds, which shared the same Fate."*

Thousands of residents found themselves homeless. The local Patriot paper *The New York Packet* reported on October 23: *"In a very short time that pleasant and wealthy town was reduced to ashes; one house only escaped the flames. Thus by the wantonness of power the third town in New York for size, elegance and wealth, is reduced to a heap of rubbish, and the once happy inhabitants . . . obliged to solicit for shelter among strangers;*

and those who lately possessed elegant and convenient dwellings, obliged to take up with such huts as they can find to defend them from the cold blasts of approaching winter."

The Hoffman House sustained minimal damage, but its attic still bears marks from the arson. Kingston's state legislature moved south to Pough-keepsie. Because Dutch settlers had favored stone buildings, reconstruction proved relatively easy. The town rebounded by the turn of the century.

In 1908, the Hoffman family sold the house to the Salvation Army. Kingston's Urban Renewal Agency bought it in 1973 and fixed its exterior. Two years later, Ginny and Pat Bradley purchased the home and that same year, the National Register of Historic Places gave the Hoffman House historical landmark status.

Restoring the house was a big undertaking. "It was in shambles," says Ginny. The Bradleys restored the building with the help of friends over the

next two years and opened for business in June 1977. Wide, shiny planks creak under the weight of visitors. Crackling fires burn in three of four dining rooms. A gigantic spinning wheel provides an old-fashioned touch positioned outside the restaurant's bathrooms.

The menu features mostly American fare with a few Mexican entrees mixed in, like a chimichanga, a quesadilla, and homemade spicy guacamole. But for the most part, the Hoffman House serves burgers, wraps, and sandwiches, like the grilled lamb and onion sandwich or the Thai chicken turkey wrap. The menu features daily pasta and quiche dishes along with salads and homemade apple cobbler, cheesecake, caramel flan, and crème brûlée. Daily specials offer choices like pork medallions in addition to mainstays like the London broil and French onion soup.

Over the last forty years, Ginny and Pat have seen Kingston change quite a bit. "When we opened, IBM was the main employer," says Ginny. IBM operated plants in Kingston, Poughkeepsie, and East Fishkill as early as 1941. The company initially manufactured aircraft cannons, then office supplies, and finally computers. IBM's presence in the Hudson Valley was not only a huge job creator, but the "Beemers" who worked there contributed to the local economy of the area as well. So when IBM laid off 2,700 people in 1993, the Hudson Valley felt it. "When they closed up and moved out we went through a few lean years," reflects Ginny.

Kingston has enjoyed a revitalization in recent years. "We've been referred to as the second Brooklyn," says Ginny. The Hoffman House serves many regulars, but draws weekend visitors from New York through all four seasons. Sitting by the fire in this charming colonial home you'll be transported back in time over a good meal.

MOHONK MOUNTAIN HOUSE

1000 MOUNTAIN REST ROAD, NEW PALTZ, NY 12561

(844) 232-7041 | WWW.MOHONK.COM

It would be most deplorable if this house should ever acquire the mercenary spirit and make the accumulation of money without higher aims the goal of its ambition.
—*Albert Smiley, October 14, 1908*

Few vacation resorts can claim they're promoting world peace. But Mohonk Mountain House, the stunning chateau and nature preserve in New Paltz, most certainly can. The property's Quaker founders promoted peace in ways big and small, from encouraging patrons to connect with nature on hikes to hosting international peace conferences that led to the establishment of The Hague's International Court of Justice and the United Nations. With both micro and macro approaches, Mohonk Mountain House has promoted serenity since 1869.

Twin brothers Albert and Alfred Smiley had always been joined at the hip. They both graduated from Oak Grove Seminary in 1845 and attended Haverford College together afterward. They looked so identical that even their mother tied a string around one twin to tell them apart as children. As mischievous adults, the men would trade their distinct pocket watches and see who could tell them apart. (This test would later be used in every single Mary-Kate and Ashley Olsen movie.) Both Albert and Alfred held firm to their Quaker values and cherished nature. They did everything together. It was only fitting, then, that they would go into business as a team.

One day in 1869, Alfred went on an excursion with his family to Paltz Point. For the first time, he saw Mohonk Lake, a half-mile-long glacier lake surrounded by trees and stone. Tavern keeper John Stokes operated a small

ten-room tavern on the bank of the lake. If any of his patrons got too unruly, Stokes reportedly chained them to the trees. After ten years, Stokes had hit hard times. When the Smiley twins expressed interest in buying the tavern and property, Stokes obliged. Despite having no experience in the hospitality industry, Albert and Alfred now owned 280 acres and set out to create a resort that reflected their values.

They started with a physical and moral makeover. They renovated Stokes Tavern to accommodate 40 guests and implemented new rules: no drinking, no dancing, and no card playing. They encouraged physical recreation, human interaction, and an appreciation of nature. They offered ten-minute prayer services after breakfast, non-denominational services on Sundays, and hymn singing in the evenings. "From the very beginning, our mission has been to provide guests with 'recreation and renewal of body, mind, and spirit in a beautiful natural setting,'" wrote Director of Marketing Nina Smiley in an email. Bit by bit, the Smiley family increased their acreage and added on to the resort. Today, the Mountain House sits on 1,200 acres and is surrounded by an additional 40,000 acres of woodlands.

For the most part, wealthy upper-class families from the East Coast constituted Mohonk's early clientele. A favorable review from early visitor Vice President Schuyler Colfax, who served in Grant's administration from 1869 to 1873, helped give Mohonk a favorable reputation. Oftentimes, patrons spent an entire summer season at Mohonk, a practice that has mostly waned in favor of shorter visits and a year-round operation.

But there remain many regulars, sometimes referred to as "Mohonkers." Mohonkers have been known to point out the smallest changes to resort staff and protest big changes. When the Mountain House decided to redo the dining hall, a group of dedicated patrons commissioned the fountain that flows out front as a memorial to the old dining hall. Another happy customer made a scale model of the Mountain House. It is on display at Mohonk today. Mohonkers don't mess around.

After a decade, the property underwent two major changes. First, Alfred left to focus on the nearby Lake Minnewaska Houses. As a result, Albert recruited his half-brother Daniel to come and manage Mohonk. Over two decades younger than Albert, Daniel would prove instrumental in Mohonk's sustainability as a premier destination. He officially began his duties in 1881.

In 1879, President Rutherford B. Hayes appointed Albert to the United States Board of Indian Commissioners, a group which advised the government on how to best work with Native American tribes and to inspect supplies sent to reservations to make sure they met requirements. The Commission seemed inadequate to Albert.

So in 1883, he hosted the first annual Lake Mohonk Conference of Friends of the Indian. He invited everyone from the Board of Indian Commissioners to participate. For the next thirty years, this conference played a part in the formation of U.S.-Native American relations and policies. The conferences acquired funds to legally protect certain groups of Native Americans and native Alaskans as well as funds for Native American college scholarships and other medical, educational, and cultural grants.

If you look around The Parlor where these conferences were held, you'll find a bust of Chief Sagonaquado. The attendees of the 1888 conferences presented the statue to Albert and his wife, Eliza. In the presentation ceremony, General Clinton Fisk praised the Smileys for their work to make up for a "century of dishonor" against Native Americans committed by "scheming land-grabbers and government contractors." They chose a bust of Sago-naquado because he embodied "the soul of honor" and exemplified "excellence in the community." Also on display in The Parlor is a painting of Chief White Eagle, a Ponta leader who lived from 1840 to 1914. "Both the painting of White Eagle and the bust of Sagonaquado were presented . . . as symbolic gifts regarding peaceful leadership (White Eagle) and honorable action (Sagonaquado)," wrote Nina.

The hotel hosted also the Lake Mohonk Conferences on International Arbitration beginning in 1895. The conferences offered a location for international matters to be discussed and resolved peacefully. Notable participants over the years included `Abdu´l-Bahá, the leader of the Baháï faith. He gave a speech at the 1912 conference titled "The Oneness of the Reality of Human Kind" and gave Albert a Persian rug as a gift to honor Albert's work for peace.

The international arbitration conferences series inspired the establishment of the Hague Court, which, in turn, inspired the formation of the United Nations. When the first Hague conference got underway, they sent a telegram from the "House in the woods in Holland" to "the house in the woods at Mohonk."

Albert died on December 2, 1912. The same year, he had been nominated for a Nobel Peace Prize. At the time, the organization did not award posthumous prizes.

Both the Conference of Friends of the Indian and the Conferences on International Arbitration continued until World War I. The Smiley family has continued its conference tradition with the Mohonk Consultations, a series on environment issues launched by Albert's grandnephew, Keith Smiley, in 1980. Their mission is "to help bring about a clearer understanding of the interrelationship of all life on earth, emphasizing the need for sustainable use of all the earth's resources, including the human community, and to support the development of practical means to do so."

Under Daniel Smiley, Mohonk Mountain House expanded while clinging to tradition. Before cars arrived on the scene, Mohonk carriages met guests

in New Paltz, and guests came with their own horses. Armed with sticks of dynamite, Daniel charged mule teams with creating eighty-five miles of carriage roads.

Complaints surged when guests started coming to Mohonk by car. Daniel officially banned cars in 1929, arguing, "Automobiles are kept out because they do not contribute to quiet and restfulness," arguing that guests do not want cars to invoke "sudden terror around projecting bluffs." The policy changed in 1933, so feel free to stop your search for a horse and buggy if you decide to visit. Drivers will note the signs that say "Slowly and

Quietly, Please" as they make the two-mile trip on the winding private road leading to Mohonk, immediately communicating that this is a place of quiet and rest, just as Daniel dictated it be almost a century ago. The roads have only been paved since the 1980s.

Mohonk's commitment to nature extends beyond its own property. The Mohonk Mountain House created the Mohonk Trust in the 1950s. This Trust established the Mohonk Preserve, a nature preserve that is legally and financially separate from the Mohonk Mountain House. The preserve is the largest private preserve in New York State.

From boating and horseback riding to golf, tennis, and hiking, Mohonk provides plenty of outdoor activities for connecting with nature. Director of Hotel Operations and fitness guru Alex Sherwood even took Bill and Hillary Clinton on a hike here a few years ago.

Mohonk Mountain House has maintained a greenhouse since 1905. It has been updated twice—first in 1976 and again in 1990. It features over 1,500 kinds of plants. The Barn Museum next to the stables dates back to 1888 and features an exhibit of antiques all used by Mohonk in the past, in addition to demonstrations in blacksmithing, carpentry, and more.

Mohonk added a spa wing in 2005. It includes a fitness center with aerobic machines and weights in addition to rooms for yoga and personal training or nutrition consultations. Services include numerous massage options, manicures, pedicures, facials, exfoliating scrubs, hair and styling services, waxing, and makeup application. The wing also includes a pool measuring 30 by 60 yards for lap swimming and recreation.

The spa even offers treatments for children age six and over who want to tag along with a parent. But children may find the game room's ping pong, air hockey, and foosball tables more interesting, or even the Kids Club that features activities for children ages two and up. Moreover, the Children's Garden features kid-friendly flora like fuzzy plants perfect for petting, a popcorn plant, a sod sofa, and a butterfly forest.

As a Quaker institution, Mohonk Mountain House's relationship with alcohol has always been on the rocks. For many years, alcohol was strictly off-limits, not allowed in public places and discouraged in private. But for those who needed their fix, one opportunistic bellhop swooped in: If guests left their shoes outside their doors to be polished, he'd slip their liquor order inside their shoes. Today, the property does create opportunities for libation lovers. "We still don't have a B-A-R," Sherwood spells out. "We have a lounge." That's code for: Keep it classy.

The name "Mohonk" has several possible translations that mean "raccoon-skin coat," "eat solid food," "place of a great tree," and "on the great sky top." The most common translation is "lake in the sky." But for many guests over the years, Mohonk has meant peace, both within and for the world.

NORTH PLANK ROAD TAVERN

30 PLANK ROAD, NEWBURGH, NY 12550

1-845-562-5031 | WWW.NORTHPLANKROADTAVERN.COM

In the earliest days of the United States, toll roads paved the way toward western expansion. Men and women traveling through the Hudson Valley toward Pennsylvania stopped at the Newburgh hotel on North Plank Road. Two hundred years later, the North Plank Road Tavern, still in operation at this spot, hosts many travelers taking a break from modern highways.

Today, Tom Costa runs the North Plank Road Tavern. "Being a tavern keeper goes back to colonial times," says Costa. "There's a historical aspect that I enjoy." From Patrick Henry to Justin Timberlake, Costa joins a long line of men keeping the tradition of tavern keeping alive.

The North Plank Road Tavern dates back to 1801. After going up or down the Hudson River, travelers took respite at the hotel/tavern before taking the plank road west.

Plank roads, constructed from wooden planks from about 1847 to 1854, seemed like a great alternative to dirt and gravel roads, which created a lot of dust under wagon wheels and horse hooves. Engineers proposed using macadam as a substitute, but this stone-based material came with high costs. George Geddes had a better solution.

An engineer from Syracuse, Geddes had engineering in his blood: His father was an engineer on the Erie and Champlain Canals. Geddes traveled to Canada in 1844 to observe its plank roads. He came back convinced they would favorably transform American transportation, touting their engineering simplicity.

Picture Lincoln logs or a rollercoaster track: Parallel lines of wood formed a road's foundation, while wooden planks laid perpendicular to these two planks formed the road. Assembly didn't even require glue or nails. The planks' own weight was enough to keep them secure.

Upon Geddes's return from Canada, he built the nation's first plank road. Called the Salina-Central Square Plank Road, the plank road stretched 12 miles and connected Syracuse to a salt work. A plank road-building boom followed. Between 1847 and 1853, New York built 3,500 miles of plank roads. These roads generally connected rural areas to canals and railroads, enabling farmers to reach new markets. For dairy farmers, plank roads proved especially transformative. Typically relegated to nearby markets because dairy doesn't last long, plank roads opened up a world of possibilities for dairy farmers.

But the plank road boom ended in 1854, when investors realized that instead of lasting for the eight to twelve years they'd been promised, plank roads needed to be replaced after four or five. Instead of pouring more money into repairs, investors cut ties. The engineering fad of the 1840s was dead.

But before plank roads got stuck in the mud, they helped make the North Plank Road Tavern a Newburgh success. By 1850, the tavern had become a rooming house. At the turn of the century, Augustus Sauer took charge of the operation. "When Prohibition came through, Mrs. Sauer just kept serving booze," reports Costa. He has found signs of the speakeasy's secret alcohol production and distribution, including a trap door and counterfeit labels.

From 1900 to 1928, Mrs. Sauer ran a seedy operation that included not only illegal alcohol production and sales during Prohibition, but also gambling and prostitution. In 1928, Sauer sold the establishment to Antoine Nixon. Nixon ran the joint until 1978, and his reign continued Sauer's tradition of rowdiness. When Costa purchased the tavern from Nixon, he took a look at Nixon's business card. "On the card [was] a naked woman holding up a martini glass. A picture says a thousand words." Nixon reportedly had dealings with the gangster Jack Diamond. It's rumored that Diamond stored his money at the North Plank Road Tavern. While today's tavern does retain the rustic charm of its nineteenth-century days, Costa has avoided the illicit activities of his predecessors. "It's never loud and crazy," he promises.

Costa has made a considerable effort to keep the tavern as it was in the nineteenth century. He consulted a city historian when redoing paneling in hopes of matching it to its original state. But one welcome change has been the addition of actual restrooms. Up until 1978, visitors relied on a brick outhouse. In particular, Costa describes the bar as "a work of art." It's two centuries old and boasts intricate woodcarvings. The walls feature Hudson River murals that date back a hundred years and some painted in "trompe l'oeil," a style where plaster is painted to look like other materials like wood and stone. "It's like you're walking into the place as it was in 1895," says Costa of the tavern's atmosphere. "You definitely feel the history of the place when you walk in."

Some of that history hangs on the wall, including an oval portrait of Mrs. Sauer, her original business sign, and framed labels of applejack whiskey

and gin, illegally produced here during Prohibition. Costa has also displayed the bottles of alcohol he uncovered in a secret hiding spot in a case on the wall.

For all its history, the North Plank Road Tavern features a very modern menu. The most popular entrees include a hanger steak and salmon, while the crab bisque and mussels are also top sellers. But the stars of the menu are the pea pancakes with roasted mushrooms. A unique dish, these pea pancakes combine egg and peas and have a batter-like consistency on the inside and a crunchy exterior. Paired with truffle-butter-soaked mushrooms, it's a dish full of unexpected flavors and textures.

The brunch menu gives a nod to its past with an Applejack Manhattan that features Applejack, bourbon, muddled raspberries, vermouth, and bitters. The drink menu also honors its former first lady with Mrs. Sauer's Cider, which combines bourbon with *domaine de canton*, ginger liqueur, apple cider, and cinnamon syrup.

The brunch menu features two types of French toast that charm the senses. The classic French toast is thick and crunchy, and paired with homemade whipped cream and an array of berries. The goat cheese French toast is truly one of a kind. An extremely thick slab of goat cheese stands between two thick slices of bread. It's more like a goat cheese panini than French toast, but it comes with beech mushrooms and black truffle fondue. Both types benefit from drizzling the tavern's own maple syrup, which perfectly complements each dish.

The kitchen uses many local products. The Black Truffle Stuffed Buratta with Vine Tomatoes, for instance, is a colorful example of the tavern's fresh ingredients and ambitious, upscale menu.

With three distinct areas—the front bar, the white tablecloth dining rooms, and an outdoor garden patio—the North Plank Road Tavern offers a historic but more polished atmosphere than the operation of yesteryear. The tavern attracts locals during the week, while the weekends bring in out-of-towners. Located off the interstate to Pennsylvania and Connecticut, travelers fill up the tavern like their counterparts did two centuries ago. Says Costa, "It's gone full cycle."

THE ORCHARD TAVERN & RESTAURANT

68 N MANNING BLVD, ALBANY, NY 12206

(518) 482-5677 | ORCHARDTAVERN.COM

Where are you going?" asked my taxi driver. "The Orchard Tavern," I responded. "A fine choice." The taxi dispatcher approved of my destination. On a rainy November afternoon I headed for one of Albany's oldest restaurants, The Orchard Tavern. Since 1903, this bar and restaurant have been serving an evolving crowd.

Located on the outskirts of town, The Orchard Tavern is a long building standing where an apple orchard once grew. In 1903, the building operated as the Bonville Saloon. Italian immigrant George Gorman purchased the saloon and rechristened it The Orchard Tavern. Father and son Jack and Michael Hickey bought the restaurant from the Gorman family. State Senator Howard Nolan and his business partner John McDaniel succeeded the Hickeys. Then came Mike and Karen Noonan, who bought the tavern in 1995 and continue to run the restaurant today.

Mike Noonan started working at The Orchard Tavern in 1980. Over the years, he took other jobs but always kept working part-time at the tavern. "I just enjoyed the atmosphere," he reflects. "It was a lot of hustle and hard work . . . but it flowed." When the opportunity to buy into the business arose, Noonan jumped.

The Noonans raised their four sons in and around the restaurant. "My earliest memories are actually here," says Brendan Noonan, the current general manager. Brendan and his brothers worked numerous jobs at the tavern throughout their upbringing. After pursuing education and job opportunities in different states, Brendan returned to Albany and runs the business alongside his parents.

The crowd at The Orchard Tavern has changed significantly over the years. When it first operated, it catered mostly to men working at the West Albany Yards. Before World War II, the yards supplied thousands of jobs. It was here that engineers constructed the first train to travel over 100 miles per hour. Known as Engine #999, it set a world record of 112 miles per hour in 1893. For comparison's sake, most Amtrak trains operate over 100 miles per hour today and max out at 150. One small room at The Orchard Tavern honors Albany's railway history with walls of old photographs arranged by railroad historian Dick Barrett.

The tavern's early customers were a rowdy bunch and known for eating bologna sandwiches and downing boilermakers (a shot of whiskey dropped into a mug of beer). Many started a tab at the beginning of the week, then cashed their paychecks at the bar and took home the difference. An armed guard was on hand to make sure transactions went smoothly, as this was a rugged group. The West Albany Yards shut down in 1954, and the tavern's clientele began to shift.

The once rambunctious bar has now become more of a family place. Alcohol sales have declined over the years. Today's customers are less likely to drink and drive, and more likely to watch their diets. The changes are "good for society," says Mike, but "not necessarily good for this business." The bar accounts for about 20 percent of The Orchard Tavern's business. Pizza sales account for about 30 percent

That's because the Orchard specializes in individual 7-by-11-inch rectangular pizza pies. They sell between 800 and 1,000 in a typical week. The dough is made in the basement on the premises in a tiny room that could more accurately be called a cave. The crust falls short of deep-dish, but it's certainly substantial. Margherita, Meat Lovers, and white pizzas grace the menu, which gets more creative with Mexican Style, Chicken Fajita, and B.L.T pizzas. Instead of the standard mozzarella, the Orchard sprinkles hearty doses of Wisconsin cheddar on its pies. "Pizza is why people come here," says Brendan. "[It's] simple but it works."

The menu also features casual fare like burgers and sandwiches in addition to pork ribs, chicken parmigiana, and spaghetti and meatballs.

The decor is decidedly unrefined. The tavern features several railroad-style rooms. Up front is the bar, where men and women sit on green cushioned backed stools or in a couple of booths below the original brown tin ceiling. The bar opens onto the main dining room with its light green ceiling, and a passage that leads to the room decorated with railway memorabilia. Plastic covers the tablecloths with a fruits-and-vegetables pattern. The dining room feels lived in and faded. A third room has more tables and chairs and an exit to the backyard, where the tavern hosts parties and events.

In 1664, the settlements of Beverwijk and Rensselaerswyck, perhaps united in their love of complicated spelling, joined to form Albany. The city officially received a charter in 1686. Just 714 people resided here in 1697, but the city grew steadily over the years. A century later, Albany officially became the capital of New York. Between 1820 and 1880 the population soared from 12,630 to 90,758. Growth has tapered since then. The 2013 census reported Albany's population as 98,424.

The Orchard Tavern sits roughly two miles away from the Empire State Plaza, where you can gaze at a collection of sculptures, marvel at the curiously designed Egg Theater, or guess what's going on inside the capitol building. If doing all that works up your appetite, head to The Orchard Tavern & Restaurant for a rectangular pizza.

PETER PRATT'S INN

673 CROTON HEIGHTS ROAD, YORKTOWN, NY 10598

(914) 962-4090 | WWW.PRATTSINN.COM

I have eaten at some of the world's top restaurants. My taste buds have enjoyed the best that New York, Paris, and Tokyo have to offer. But I ate one of the best meals of my entire life one hour north of Manhattan at Peter Pratt's Inn.

Located in Yorktown, the restaurant exists in a former barn that dates back to 1780. The structure changed hands a few times in the nineteenth century. In the early twentieth century, publisher Halsey Wilson bought the house and created the town of Croton Heights when he sold plots of land to his literary friends.

In 1926 the house became an inn. Russian Count Victor Kotschoubey bought the property in the 1940s, and it became a destination for his many famous friends, including members of the Vanderbilt and Duncan Hines families. In 1965, Peter and Janet Pratt bought the inn and transformed it into a restaurant. Their chef son, Jonathan Pratt, runs it today.

On a rainy Saturday night, the basement restaurant's twinkling lights and low lighting offered a warm escape from the elements. A fireplace draws guests in the winter, and the patio attracts visitors on warmer days. Inside, a few prints and paintings decorate the walls without overwhelming them. White tablecloths complete the elegant atmosphere. Guests enter via a green door under a triangular entryway on the side of the home.

Under Jonathan's parents, Peter Pratt's Inn featured a fine dining French experience. But now under Jon, the restaurant offers a stunning farm-to-table menu featuring local products. He changes the menu often, incorporating fresh tomatoes, corn, and kale from local Meadows Farm. Months after dining at the restaurant, I'm still craving the seven-tomato burrata:

Seven varieties of tomatoes, each with their own distinctive taste, join the soft, creamy buratta with a perfect helping of olive oil. The tomato basil soup is inspired, a smoky creamy sensation that remained hot even after fifteen minutes on the table.

The quesadilla appetizer features thin, crispy Peking duck with sour cream, plum sauce, and scallion served between toasted flatbreads. The short rib pizza is made with a wholewheat crust. The Belgian Waffle, served with vanilla ice cream and caramelized apples, features the "Deep Deep Dark, Undercover Special, Reserve Can't Touch This White Oak Farm Maple Syrup." With a name like that, how could you not try it? The kitchen also makes its own root beer for root beer floats and its own gluten-free ice cream.

Because the menu changes frequently, these items may not be available when you visit. Expect to be impressed, however, as it's clear that Jonathan knows what he's doing in the kitchen. The menu's affordable for the quality and scale of items offered. While you can't sleep at the inn, there's a plan in the works to restore the nine bedrooms and bathrooms above the restaurant.

Over the years, many employees have reported seeing the ghost of an American soldier from the Revolutionary War. This makes sense, since a battle did take place nearby during the American Revolution: Known as the Battle of Pines Bridge (May 14, 1781), this was an important engagement for the Continental Army's black soldiers. Rhode Island led the colonies as the first to recruit free black men and slaves into the Continental Army. (See the entry on Fraunces Tavern on page 27 for more information.) These 130 new recruits made up the First Rhode Island Regiment. The army promised the slaves in this regiment freedom at the end of their service.

On April 15, 1781, the regiment took up the task of defending the northern bank of the Croton River, which flowed into the Hudson River. A month later, British forces attacked the First Rhode Island, outnumbering them two to one. Fourteen men perished, 100 suffered injuries, and 30 wound up as British prisoners. The British sold most of these prisoners back into slavery in the British West Indies. Colonel Greene Road, which leads to Peter Pratt's Inn, is named for the leader of the First Rhode Island Regiment, who died in this battle.

If you follow Colonel Greene Road to Peter Pratt's Inn, you're sure to have one of the best meals of your life.

THE STONE HOUSE BED & BREAKFAST

476, OLD ROUTE 209, HURLEY, NY 12443

845-339-4041 | WWW.HURLEYSTONEHOUSE.COM

There are a lot of old buildings in New York. But if you want to visit the oldest building you can actually sleep in, head for The Stone House Bed & Breakfast in Hurley, New York. Owners Sam and Nadia Scoogins believe that their bed and breakfast, built in 1705, is the oldest place you can legally rest your head in the Empire State.

The Esopus Native Americans are the earliest known occupants of this property. An archaeological dig conducted on this land by the State University of New York at New Paltz in the 1970s revealed artifacts from 2000 BCE. Those artifacts are now on display at the New Paltz campus of the State University of New York.

In the 1600s, Dutch colonists moved into the area. Among those immigrants was the Kool family, who built the house that has become known as The Stone House. "The oldest part of the building that's still standing [was built] between 1705 and 1720 the architectural historians tell us," says Sam Scoogins. The house is part of Hurley's Historic District, which includes many Dutch houses from the early eighteenth century. The Hurley Preservation Commission protects the exteriors of these historic homes but allows citizens to alter the interiors.

The Scooginses purchased the property in 2008 and turned the two-family home into a bed and breakfast. Sam's parents ran a B and B in England, and he grew up in a big, old house; The Stone House Bed & Breakfast merges both facets of his background. "We were attracted to the old stone houses because they were European and reminded us of where we were from," explains Sam. "We renovated and installed, you know, lots of bathrooms," he explains. "I know more about American bathrooms than I ever wanted to know."

The house retains its Dutch roots. "It's from that Dutch period even though the British had taken over," explains Sam. "It's older than the United States." That means jambless fireplaces, wide wooden planked floors, and a Dutch front door. Dutch doors are essentially two doors in one, offering top and bottom doors for semi-closure. This house's door includes a dolphin doorknocker and a key from 1869.

The charming house features the detailed design work by the Scooginses, who both had experience with art and flipping houses before embarking on this venture. Antiques like a spinning wheel and the nightgown of a long-lost resident fill corners. Nadia compared the process to decorating "a doll's house, but a lot bigger." From Victorian claw-foot tubs and blue and white Dutch Delft tiles, the owners have accented each room with aesthetic details that mix history with art.

The house sits on a hill that slopes down to the Esopus Creek. Sam and Nadia own the two acres that the house sits on and four acres across the street, where oral history suggests that slave graves exist but have never been confirmed. Bears and coyotes have been heard in the area. If you look out the rear window toward the river, you'll see land that is now a hub for sustainable farming. With the Culinary Institute of America nearby in Hyde Park, guests can benefit from a number of great restaurants led by CIA graduates in the area who rely on organic, sustainable farms for their ingredients.

"We're here because of the location," says Nadia. In addition to great restaurants, guests clamor for the outdoor activities that the location provides, from hiking and biking to skiing and kayaking. The Stone House is strictly BYOK (Bring Your Own Kayak) so if you want to explore the Esopus Creek, strap a vessel on your car.

Fall brings the most guests to The Stone House, many from Brooklyn, New York. "The house attracts interesting people," muses Sam. Friendships and contacts have been made over a communal breakfast. "It's totally the best part," Nadia says of these interactions.

Guests can enjoy a three-course breakfast together in the living room. A typical breakfast might begin with homemade bread and granola, followed by a mushroom frittata and fruit salad. Nadia does most of the cooking and has collected a handful of recipes in a book that includes her instructions for gluten-free oat and rye breads in addition to almond muffins, a frittata, and baked apples with cranberry coulis.

A small, cozy operation, The Stone House Bed & Breakfast is lovingly decorated and cared for and offers a historic place to rest your head.

THE THAYER HOTEL

674 THAYER ROAD, WEST POINT, NY 10996

(845) 446-4731 | WWW.THETHAYERHOTEL.COM

The Thayer Hotel opened on June 3, 1926, as part of West Point's U.S. Military Academy. The school built this Gothic structure overlooking the Hudson River to house visiting dignitaries and important guests of the school. Originally owned and operated by the federal government, it is now owned by a group of West Point graduates.

The hotel is named after Sylvanus Thayer, one of the most instrumental and longest-serving superintendents of the military academy. Thayer graduated from Dartmouth College in 1807. Excellent marks earned him the

distinction of valedictorian. As an undergrad, he explored his interests in foreign affairs and military strategy by studying the exploits of Napoleon. President James Madison nominated Thayer to study at the military academy. Applications to West Point must include a nomination from a member of Congress, a governor, the vice president, or a distinguished member of the armed forces.

When Thayer arrived in 1808, he found a school lacking basic structure and organization. The school didn't have a formal curriculum. Professors bestowed graduation upon students at random times at their personal discretion. Thayer graduated in just one year.

He went on to fight the British in the War of 1812. He was in charge of directing and defending a base in Norfolk, Virginia. For his ability to defend this fort from British control, the army elevated Thayer to the rank of brevet major. This promotion comes with higher distinction, but no pay raise.

After the war, Thayer toured Europe's military schools on behalf of West Point's Military Academy to gather fodder for reforms. He returned to the United States after two years armed with ideas. Under his sixteen-year reign as superintendent, the school became a well-structured machine for churning out well-trained cadets. For this, Thayer is known as "The Father of the Military Academy."

Thayer retired from West Point in 1833. During the next thirty years he worked as an army engineer and endowed Dartmouth with the Thayer School of Engineering. He retired in 1863 at the rank of brigadier general and died in 1872. Five decades later, West Point honored its premier forefather with The Thayer Hotel.

The Thayer Hotel hosted the Iranian Hostage Crisis victims upon their return to the United States in 1981 after 444 days in captivity. The hotel increased its staff and emptied the hotel of other guests to provide a comfortable, private environment for these 52 Americans to recover and reunite with their families. The Thayer Hotel invited the former hostages back in 2011 on the thirtieth anniversary of their return to American soil.

The Thayer Hotel offers a number of dining options on site. MacArthur's Riverview Restaurant is known for its Sunday Brunch featuring unlimited champagne, mimosas, and Bloody Marys, and its seafood offerings. The hotel also features two bar/lounges. The first, Patton's Tavern, provides simple fare in a casual setting next to MacArthur's. The second, Zulu Time, is named for the way that the military tells time. Also known as Greenwich Mean Time, Zulu Time is the same in every location worldwide, a necessity when talking military strategy across the globe.

Staying or dining at The Thayer Hotel is likely to be one of the safest hospitality experiences of your life. If you have any trouble, throngs of young cadets and seasoned military experts are nearby to help. So pass the security check, drive on to campus, and unwind at this historic hotel on the Hudson River.

INDEX BY YEAR

ACKNOWLEDGMENTS

I would like to thank my agent Anne Marie O'Farrell and Amy Lyons at Globe Pequot for the opportunity to write this book. Many thanks also to the proprietors, publicists, managers, and historians who shared their time and knowledge with me as I researched these establishments. Infinite thanks as always to my wonderful family, especially Bonnie Brienza.

PHOTO CREDITS

Cover credits: Front, clockwise from top left: Courtesy of Delmonico's; Grand Central Oyster Bar & Restaurant © Michael Freeman/Alamy; © Thinkstock. com; Courtesy of Mohonk Mountain House; Courtesy of Keens Steakhouse; © Thinkstock. Back, clockwise from top left: Mohonk Mountain House (c) Doug Schneider/Alamy; Courtesy of the Fraunces Tavern Museum; © Thinkstock; Courtesy of the Grand Central Oyster Bar & Restaurant; Courtesy of P.J. Clarke's.

Pages vi, 2: © Thinkstock
Page ix, x: Licensed by Shutterstock.com
Pages 6, 8, 10: Courtesy of Barbetta
Page 13: Photo by Ignacio Gómez Cuesta | Via Flickr
Pages 18, 20, 22, 23: Courtesy of Delmonico's
Pages 24, 25: Ear Inn: Courtesy of Laura Brienza
Pages 29, 31, 34: Courtesy of the Fraunces Tavern Museum
Pages 37, 39: Courtesy of Frying Pan
Pages 41, 43, 45, 47: Courtesy of the Grand Central Oyster Bar & Restaurant
Pages 50, 55, 58: Courtesy of Laura Brienza
Pages 62, 64, 66: Courtesy of Keens Steakhouse
Pages 67, 68, 70: Courtesy of Lombardi's Pizza
Pages 72, 75, 77: Courtesy of Bryan Thatcher
Pages 79, 80, 82: Courtesy of Laura Brienza
Pages 85, 87, 88: Courtesy of Old Homestead Steakhouse
Pages 93, 95: Courtesy of Peter Sylvester
Pages 96, 99: Courtesy of Laura Brienza
Pages 101, 103: Courtesy of Pete's Tavern
Pages 105, 107, 108: Courtesy of P.J. Clarke's
Pages 110, 113: Courtesy of Laura Brienza
Pages 117, 118, 120–21: Courtesy of Tavern on the Green
Pages 125, 127, 128, 130: Courtesy of Waldorf Astoria New York

Pages 133, 135: Courtesy of Laura Brienza

Pages 138, 140: Courtesy of Laura Brienza

Pages 142, 143, 145: Courtesy of Ferdinando's Focacceria

Page 147: Courtesy of Monte's

Page 149: Courtesy of Laura Brienza

Pages 151: The 2013 Nathan's Hot Dog Eating Contest | Courtesy Major League Eating

Page 152: 2013 Champion Joey Chestnut, left, defeats Takeru Kobayashi, right | Courtesy Major League Eating

Page 155: 2013 Nathan's Famous Hot Dog Eating Contest champions Joey Chestnut, left, and Sonya Thomas, right | Courtesy Major League Eating

Pages 157, 159: Courtesy of Peter Luger Steak House

Page 160: Courtesy of Laura Brienza

Pages 163, 164, 165: Courtesy of The Beer Garden at Bohemian Hall

Pages 166, 168: Courtesy of Neir's Tavern

Pages 171, 172, 173: Courtesy of Tweed's Restaurant and Buffalo Bar

Page 177: Photo by Ben Borkowski | Via Flickr

Page 179: Courtesy of Yankee Tavern

Pages 182, 184, 185: Courtesy of Killmeyer's Old Bavarian Inn

Pages 191, 194: Courtesy of The '76 House

Pages 197, 198, 199: Courtesy of The 1850 House Inn & Tavern

Pages 200, 201: Courtesy of the Cromwell Manor Historic Inn

Page 202: Courtesy of Laura Brienza

Pages 205, 206, 207: Courtesy of Hoffman House

Pages 210, 213, 215: Courtesy of Mohonk Mountain House

Pages 216, 219: Courtesy of North Plank Road Tavern

Page 220: Courtesy of Laura Brienza

Pages 222: Courtesy of Daniel Berman

Page 224: Courtesy of Laura Brienza

Page 226: Courtesy of Laura Brienza

Page 229: Courtesy of The Stone House Bed & Breakfast

Pages 231, 233: Courtesy of The Thayer Hotel

ABOUT THE AUTHOR

Laura Brienza is a writer from New Jersey. Her book *Discovering Vintage Washington, DC* was published by Globe Pequot in 2015. Her plays have been developed and produced at the Kennedy Center, the Lark Play Development Center, Luna Stage, Carnegie Stage, and more. She also writes for film and TV. In her spare time, Laura enjoys racing triathlons. She splits her time between New York City and Los Angeles.